LETTING GO OF LONELINESS

Founder of the national and international organisations Shape and Interlink, which forge links between the creative arts and the disadvantaged, Gina Levete is a writer now based in London.

Letting Go of Loneliness

A Positive Approach

Gina Levete

ELEMENT
Shaftesbury, Dorset ● Rockport, Massachusetts
Brisbane, Queensland

© Gina Levete 1993

Published in Great Britain in 1993 by
Element Books Limited
Longmead, Shaftesbury, Dorset

Published in the USA in 1993 by
Element Inc
42 Broadway, Rockport, MA 01966

Published in Australia in 1993 by
Element Books Limited for
Jacaranda Wiley Limited
33 Park Road, Milton, Brisbane 4064

Cover design by Max Fairbrother
Designed by Roger Lightfoot
Typeset by Colset Private Ltd, Singapore
Printed and bound in Great Britain by
Dotesios Ltd, Trowbridge, Wiltshire

British Library Cataloguing in Publication
data available

Library of Congress Cataloging in Publication
data available

ISBN   1-85230-398-0

Contents

For the human heart

Introduction

Many of us will experience loneliness at some time in our lives: rich or poor, young or old. Loneliness can be one of the causes of a number of social problems or illnesses. More often its effects are less dramatic but equally significant – feelings of isolation and demoralization.

Loneliness seems to be a particularly Western phenomenon. Despite the wealth of counselling and social support available today, loneliness is extremely common. However, it is little discussed. Why? Perhaps it is because we all feel vulnerable. Perhaps it is because the subject is considered too vast and complex – where do you begin? But, unless the problem is confronted, those suffering can enter a downward spiral.

At present the word 'lonely', and the condition it describes, carry a stigma. People are often hesitant to acknowledge their loneliness to others. If they do, they may be associated with being 'difficult', a social failure, someone looking for a relationship. Admitting to it may make others step even further away.

The well-meaning but sometimes misplaced sensitivity of social support organizations does not always help. Recognizing that loneliness is a very real problem, the World Health Organisation and the UK Department of Health and Social Security prefer to describe it as 'social isolation'. This they feel is a more acceptable phrase. As one man commented, ' "Social isolation" sounds like a germ, but then I expect that's what they think we've got.'

We are all wary of addressing the subject – the lonely person, the media, the support organizations. Until we acknowledge and recognize it for what it is, a common

1

problem, people will continue to feel isolated and often ashamed of being lonely.

This book is written for people who experience loneliness; it can be most usefully followed as a course. Each chapter looks at loneliness from a different perspective, and suggests ways to confront and work through it. Loneliness need not be seen as an entirely negative condition. From this experience can grow self-reliance, insight and wisdom. The first stage is to define and come to terms with our own loneliness, looking inwards before seeking external solutions, in order to build a firm foundation. Then, when the time is right, we can step out.

CHAPTER ONE

An Overall View of Loneliness

Loneliness is not an 'ism', an illness or an addiction. The age of technology enables us now to be universally aware of each other's lives, yet its development also separates us. Many more people will find themselves working or spending longer stretches of time alone. While we need to stop thinking that being alone is a last resort, something to be feared, we also need to understand the natural human need for love and friendship and not judge those who say they feel lonely.

Many mistakes in forming relationships occur through the fear of being alone. Perhaps education can play a more significant role in helping young people from primary school age upwards not to be afraid of being alone, or regard it as 'not normal'. Often the 'loner' in school is looked upon both by pupils and staff as strange. Group pressure begins at an early age and continues through life. (*See also* the section on teenage loneliness in Chapter 10.)

Children need the encouragement of parents and teachers to enjoy playing and working alone. Teenagers need to be given opportunities to discuss in the classroom both the positive and negative aspects of this condition, presenting their own ideas on how to support lonely people. Facing this subject head-on from an early age will help to eliminate its stigma.

The media in its many forms has the greatest potential to change public attitudes. Present television and film commercials nearly always portray success as being surrounded by admiring people, walking hand in hand, a happy family or the perfect retired couple – none of which is wrong, provided it is balanced with images of people enjoying life alone. The tourist industry does nothing to help the single person's self-esteem. Indeed, it does its best to make the lone holiday-goer feel like a second-class citizen. If he or she wants a single room, there is an extra charge. You can assume that when it comes to mealtimes in the restaurant the lone person, particularly if female, will be put in a faraway corner. Attitudes such as these pervade many aspects of our present-day society. They need changing. Loneliness is nothing to be ashamed of; our attitude towards it is.

Before beginning to look at the subject from different perspectives it may be useful to consider the meaning of some of the words used to describe loneliness. Words themselves often help us to transform situations.

The Oxford Dictionary defines lonely as 'sad because one lacks friends' or 'solitary without companions'. 'Sad because one lacks friends' is a stark image, whereas 'solitary without companions' conjures up a gentler state. Similarly the phrases 'to be lonely' or 'to be alone' create different pictures. The first is a cry for support from others; the latter indicates a degree of self-sufficiency, even preference. The basis for our exploration of loneliness is the word 'solitaire', defined as 'a diamond or gem set by itself'.

'A diamond or gem set by itself' – each of us is just that. We come into the world alone, and we leave alone. Surely, to be alone is part of the natural cycle of life, only we have been conditioned to see it as otherwise. Social pressures encourage us to believe that to enjoy life we should be out there partying with others, or with the perfect companion. If things are not working out, then these images of what 'should' be happening can leave us feeling lonely, demoralized and apart. No less so for those who have joined the wrong party, and stay on to avoid being on their own.

The inner qualities we all possess, which equip us to be at peace with our own company, often lie dormant beneath a constant bombardment of internal anxiety and external pressures. The present-day intellectual separation from so many natural processes has meant that 'alone' has turned into 'lonely'.

Just as an oak tree may have to stand by itself in a field, we too may have to stand alone at some point in our lives.

Should this happen for reasons which at the time are unclear to us, the situation can be eased by standing back and looking at it objectively. If we can reconnect to the thread which leads us back to our centre, the tranquil innermost part, we may find a space where there is peace, where we can step beyond conditioned boundaries. This book explores different ways to find the thread that can lead through the labyrinth and out the other side.

Working our way out of loneliness requires effort and a sense of purpose. Look upon the task as serious and worth while, a course you are embarking upon. This book is the manual to help you through the course. It may be easier to read the book and then follow the suggestions, chapter by chapter, moving on only when each idea has been thoroughly explored. The suggested approaches can apply to any situation, be it acute or less severe. Translate them to fit your particular circumstances.

DEFINING LONELINESS

Defining precisely what loneliness means to us is an essential first step, and one that will bring immediate benefit. We start to distance ourselves from the problem, becoming the observer rather than the participant. However, it is not just a question of saying 'Well it's simple, I have no friends', 'I long for a partner', 'I miss my wife', 'I've always been lonely inside . . .'. We have to look deeply and thoughtfully at the ways loneliness affects our physical and mental well-being, our daily life, and how we interact with others, clarifying some of the confusion that can surround the problem.

Taking the decision to draw up an honest definition may demand effort of will and mental discipline. Nevertheless it is a worthwhile and healthy resolve. Head-on confrontation with feelings of loneliness is often avoided, perhaps because they appear unclear or overlap with more easily understood emotions. Acutely lonely people may learn not to attend to their loneliness by hermetically sealing themselves into an isolated state of being. This protective mechanism may ease the situation, but can result in the negative effects of loneliness manifesting themselves under other guises. (*See* Chapter 7, Coping with Acute Loneliness.)

Before considering how to define the problem it will be useful to look at the two main kinds of loneliness as well as the more obvious factors that can contribute to it. Loneliness has two aspects – internal and external. One invariably results in the other, so to a greater or lesser degree both affect us.

Inner Loneliness

People suffering from profound inner loneliness often feel a deep-rooted sense of isolation or alienation, feeling apart from everyone and everything, sealed in their condition, and cut off socially. In this state it is hard to reach out for help and friendship. Traumatic childhood experiences, lack of affection at an early age, or other damaging situations which leave little or no confidence and self-esteem, can be causes for this condition. The state may manifest itself as deep depression, sorrow, unspecified physical and mental symptoms, apathy, even addictions. As one person said, 'Cigarettes and chocolate become a replacement for friends'.

For many of us the effects of inner loneliness are not so acute but nevertheless cause distress. Anxieties such as perceiving oneself to be the outsider, not belonging, harbouring unspecified wishes to fill a void, or bewilderment and guilt at feeling lonely, despite being surrounded by family or friends, are common worries which cause many a painful sigh.

External Loneliness

This often results from social, circumstantial or environmental conditions. Social factors could be the loss of a loved one, the lack of a partner, a divorce, a destructive relationship, or missing the children who have fled the nest. There could be circumstances beyond our immediate control, such as an illness or disability that leaves us vulnerable or house-bound, becoming elderly and frail, being isolated because of caring for an ill dependant, displaced and struggling to make roots in a new country, the victim of racial harassment, adjusting to unemployment or redundancy, homelessness or poor accommodation, poverty. In addition, there are contributory environmental factors like inadequate transport in rural areas, traffic-congested cities or towns, lack of access for disabled people, few green spaces, inadequate facilities for families or young people, fear of crime – everyday conditions which affect many people. (*See also* Chapter 11.)

Many people face none of these difficulties yet still experience loneliness. Those who live in more privileged circumstances often feel ashamed or diffident about being this way with no obvious reasons, so rather than seek help there is a tendency to suffer in silence. Never feel guilty or ashamed of being lonely.

So how is it possible to work through this condition? The first step is to define the problem for ourselves by drawing up an honest assessment of our situation. This written assessment will be a reference point for the work to follow.

Exercise: Defining your loneliness

Allow yourself half an hour or more and find a quiet space to be in. Start by acknowledging inwardly or out loud to yourself that loneliness is a problem and you intend to tackle it: 'Yes, loneliness is a problem for me.' Write down all the reasons you perceive to be its cause. Slow down. Keep reminding yourself there is no right or wrong. Self-criticism plays no part in this assessment. You are simply drawing up an honest outline.

Then, write down your thoughts and observations under the following categories: mental effects, physical effects, social effects, fears. Under the heading 'fears' write about any that may directly or indirectly be connected with loneliness. List anything that you feel would solve the various difficulties written about – solutions from the seemingly impossible to the more realistic.

Ask yourself about the feelings. Is it largely internal or external? How far back does it go? Were you lonely as a child? Are you an inward- or outward-looking person? Are you shy or over-effusive? Do you find it easy to smile and accept people as they are; or are you upset if your sincere beliefs are not reciprocated by others? Do you have low self-esteem or do you regard yourself as a valuable human being? Has your sense of humour been eroded by this condition? Has dissatisfaction with your appearance anything to do with being shy or lacking in confidence? If so try to explain it to yourself. Are you aware of any nervous mannerisms such as not being able to look people in the face, finding it difficult to smile spontaneously, an inability to keep still when with others? Finally, are there any positive aspects of this experience?

Having had the courage to make this assessment, put it away for the time being. Deliberately forget it. Allow yourself to sit peacefully for a few minutes. Don't do anything, just let the mind and body rest, listen to the silence or the sounds in the street, let go of everything and feel your breathing.

The following day put aside half an hour. Read your assessment and reflect upon it. Cross out anything that now appears not to be the real issue, and add anything that does.

Under the various headings, note the observations which are of particular interest to you. Decide whether one of these aspects will be the starting point for tackling the problem. Refer to this outline as you explore the rest of the book. It will enable you to evaluate any changes that occur, as you work your way through this course.

CONFRONTING YOUR FEELINGS

Often fear of loneliness rather than the actual experience causes us to make wrong decisions. Imagined loneliness is a real bogey, particularly with regard to relationships.

To avoid loneliness, hasty partnerships may be established, or panic moves made, that lead us in the wrong direction. We may even find ourselves 'buying' imaginary security, anything to prevent living alone. In truth, there is no such thing as security. Everything, including human beings, changes from moment to moment.

However stable a relationship appears to be, if one partner silently harbours imagined fears of loneliness, he or she is vulnerable, likely to compromise from fear of being abandoned. Sensing this, consciously or unconsciously the other person may become dominant. Fear of loneliness may thus lead to a destructive relationship.

Ideally, if all of us could have a period of time on our own ('sticking out' the lonely bits) before committing ourselves to any partnership, there would be a greater chance of relationships being equal. Knowing how to survive and enjoy life as an independent and inwardly self-sufficient being or, as one described it, 'a solo-orientated person', we are of more use to our partner and ourselves.

Imagined fear is nearly always worse than the reality. Loneliness can be horrible but it need not remain that way. In some cases it can be overcome, in others transformed to the gentler state of 'aloneness'. Most of us will know someone who truly comes into their own when the pain and grief of losing a partner has begun to heal. If through fear of loneliness you have been prevented from pursuing a course of action you believe to be right, grit your teeth, let go, take the plunge and don't be afraid.

Many human beings, of different ages, different sizes, different circumstances, different backgrounds and outlook, all experience variations of this common and neglected problem. Working our way out of loneliness requires commitment. Don't let it become a familiar hump which you carry around. You are not attached to this state by an invisible thread.

The first stage was acknowledgement. Stage two is confrontation, observing how this condition affects us physically and mentally. When we first experience loneliness, our immediate reaction can be to seek external solutions, either through joining clubs or pursuing various activities that will bring social contact. We may devote time and thought to all the things we think we should be doing to help ourselves, but then fail to follow through because of lack of confidence or heart. And if remedies are applied before taking inward stock, our unresolved fears are likely to reappear, and the search for new solutions may become even more hectic.

In the first instance we need to muster the courage to stay

with the problem and sit with it, observing and accepting the resulting physical and mental sensations. Accepting these feelings does not imply for evermore surrendering to them. On the contrary, by looking at them objectively, we are distancing ourselves from them and not allowing them to whirl us about as if we were in a tumble dryer.

Should the mind become swamped by negative emotions, an effective way to calm it is to adopt an approach similar to forms of basic meditation. Some readers may recoil at the word 'meditation', feeling that a set of religious beliefs is about to be imposed upon them. A common misunderstanding is that meditation (which can mean simply allowing yourself a time of quiet stillness) can only be practised within the context of a religion. Chapter 5 looks at the benefits of being able to still the mind and occasionally 'switch off', and the exercise below will help you to achieve this. Other exercises to help overcome a negative state of mind are suggested in Chapter 7, Coping with Acute Loneliness.

Exercise: Coping with negative emotions

When overwhelmed by an acute sensation of loneliness, or any other disturbing emotions for that matter, withdraw into yourself for a few moments. If it is possible, sit down with the back held in an upright position, the eyes gently closed or half closed. In a public place or with others adapt the practice to fit the situation.

Breathe in deeply to the count of four, and exhale to the count of six or until all the breath has been expelled. Breathe in through the nostrils and draw the breath down to the belly. The abdomen is now being filled with air. Exhale, pressing down on the abdomen so that all the breath is expelled up and back through the nostrils. The abdomen expands and contracts like a pair of bellows. Gently and deeply breathe in and out four or five times. Then allow the breathing to resume its natural rhythm. Focus your attention on the breath. Be in each moment. Too often the mind is either in the past in replay, or way ahead writing a script which may never happen.

As the breathing becomes softer, observe the thoughts passing through the mind, the fears, anxiety, confusion, as well as the internal chatter that may be going on. Allow it all to be there, rather than suppressing it or trying to work things out. Just surrender, let go of having to do something, or be brave. Surprisingly, surrendering mentally to any sensation of hurt nearly always brings relief. At this stage it may help to speak to yourself either aloud or inwardly. Hard as this may be, try to express how you feel with humour however ironic. 'Ouch, this is so painful it hurts! . . .' 'I'm just one bundle of negativity! . . .' Now be silent. Listen to the silence or the sounds outside. Start breathing softly and deeply again as you remind yourself that the problem of loneliness is a common one and bears no reflection upon you. Breathe in goodwill to yourself, and breathe out goodwill to all other people who are also experiencing loneliness at that very moment.

Acute and overwhelming states usually pass quite quickly. If this approach is practised when they do occur, you will derive strength from knowing you can deal with them in this way. There is you, and there are transitory negative thoughts passing like clouds over a clear blue sky. Our true nature is the clear blue sky.

COMING TO TERMS WITH THE SITUATION

Stage three is to begin to come to terms with ourselves and our situation. To do this it may help to refer back to the exercise at the beginning of the chapter where you started to define your feelings. Now take this further and start to assess them. We are not concerned here with right or wrong, just with the way things are.

Exercise: Assessing the situation

Reflect calmly on your loneliness and what you might do about it. Is it likely that because of your make-up there may always be some sense of being apart? If so, can you come to terms with this fact? Will it help to work on various aspects of your personality by yourself or do you need the help of others? For example, on your own can you work through shyness or that sense of apartness? Can you learn to be less effusive or anxious to be liked? If friendship or partnership is your need, consider carefully where to begin looking.

Responsible friendship agencies need not be thought of as a last resort, for they may be a sensible and logical way to meet new people (*see* Chapter 12). Or do you need to work through your loneliness first?

Are you a person who finds it difficult to make a lasting commitment either in friendship or partnership? If so, will you begin to accept this fact and work from there on your own? Do you need help? If circumstances which cannot be changed are the cause of loneliness, can you work around them, perhaps with the help of a counsellor or therapist? If you are elderly, and suffer through the loss of a loved one, is this perhaps because of an unconscious tryst?

Are you young and in danger of becoming a hermit because you have been hurt? If so perhaps the time has come to take the plunge and interact with other people again, even if this takes monumental effort and courage. Enjoying life with others can be looked upon as an act of generosity on your part.

Are you a loner secretly longing to be a joiner? Consider carefully whether this is possible. Forcing oneself to be a joiner may work with compromises, otherwise it can be even more lonely and very tiring. Are you someone who has tried everything and yet still remains lonely? If so, is there a need to come gracefully to terms with this, and view it from a different perspective, utilizing the condition as an opportunity for self-development?

Make a pledge to yourself not to retreat into a sad shell if the route you decide to follow does not work out at first. View failed efforts with humour. 'That was the worst, most boring evening of my life, never again!' 'Therapy – she just doesn't have enough life experience. Maybe I should be the therapist!' Make a pledge to yourself not to be downhearted.

Finding the right recipe requires trying out a number of ingredients. The following chapters suggest some of the basic ones needed.

CHAPTER TWO

Perceptions of Yourself

THE 'SMALL ME' AND THE 'BIG I'

We have the choice of being dominated by 'small me' thinking or living as part of the 'Big I'. This concept was originally put forward by Shunryu Suzuki-roshi in a beautiful book *Zen Mind, Beginner's Mind*. Shunryu Suzuki-roshi speaks of 'one mind only' – the Big mind – the original mind which comes out of emptiness rather than the relative mind which sets itself up in relation to other things. It is useful to take this concept as a basis for letting go of loneliness and negative patterns of thought.

Our conditioned limited thinking is the small me mind. Small me is unaware of the unlimited energy within, the energy which gives us the power to take control of our lives in a manner which expresses our true nature. Small me thinking is in continual conflict with itself: what I ought to be, what I ought not to be, what others should be, what they should not be. We feel isolated, having to battle against the forces of nature and be in control of everything. Rarely with the small me mind are we able to live spontaneously. In order to protect ourselves we either hang on to the past or leapfrog to an imagined future. Small me mind tends to point the finger of blame. We perceive ourselves to be victims. Unwittingly we lock ourselves in through fear, mistrust or a sense of helplessness. In so doing, the unlimited energy within manifests itself as patterns of negative thought rather than positive power. A negative mind is a lonely mind. It cuts us off from the support we long for.

Our original universal mind is the silent Big I. Unconditioned, it comes out of emptiness, open to everything and everyone. Its thinking is spacious, generous, non-judgmental, wise and compassionate. It flows with what is and works from there rather than trying to manipulate life like the small me mind does.

To express our true nature we have to let go of the small me mind and reconnect to the Big I mind. When we choose to live and think as the Big I, we develop an unshakeable heart, one that weathers both the good and the not so good times. With the Big I we learn to live courageously, with grace and dignity. We are in touch with reality. We recognize our independence and at the same time our universal interdependence.

YOUR SELF-PORTRAIT

To release the Big I, we need to look at our perceptions of ourselves. The images we have of ourselves become distorted if we build them around negative beliefs and ignore our positive qualities. Is your self-portrait true or false? A negative image will colour the way you project yourself, and the way other people respond to you. Appearance, character, personality, how we imagine others see us, and a flickering awareness of an inner essence, our true nature, these are all the components of a self-portrait. Understanding the perceptions we have about ourselves, and the way we project those images, is another step away from loneliness.

Appearance

Few of us are content with the way we look. Even the most beautiful or handsome person will tell you so. We judge our looks by comparison with others, influenced by society's approved stereotypes – which we often try to emulate. Emulation need not be seen as negative. Profound systems of thought and others' ideas and creations are there for us to enjoy and learn from. Comparison is dangerous only if we hand over our own powers of discernment. Then our own

individual expression or characteristics may be misinter-
preted, ignored or repressed by a surfeit of socially acceptable
or media-approved images that we strive to imitate. It is hard
not to be influenced by the media's edicts of beauty and fashion:
attractive, unattractive, worth following up, not worth a
second glance. As you begin to consider how you see yourself
it may be surprising to discover how much feelings about
appearance can contribute to the condition of loneliness.

If there are aspects of your appearance which make you
feel at a real disadvantage, it helps to acknowledge the
situation out loud, preferably looking in a mirror. Doing
this brings a feeling of release and strength. Then perhaps
there are choices – either peacefully and confidently to
accept the way you look or, if you prefer, and provided
it is wise, change the perceived flaw. There is no right or
wrong attached to such choices, simply what is right for you.
The exercise below helps you to look at yourself clearly.

Exercise: Assessing appearance

List in two columns under 'like' and 'don't like', aspects of
your appearance which either give you confidence or bother
you. For example:

Like	Don't Like
Great breasts	Breasts too big
Well built	Pot belly
Masculine	Too hairy and macho looking
Petite	Too small
Interesting wrinkles	Wrinkles
Nicely rounded	Too fat
Slender	Too thin
Designer stubble	Never look shaven
Curly hair	Fuzzy hair
Moustache	Balding

Do you see yourself largely in terms of 'likes' and 'don't likes'?
Are you concerned with how you think others see you?
If the negative aspects outweigh the positive ones ask yourself why. Take time to consider the question. Is insecurity
the reason? Invariably the roots of insecurity are sown

during our formative years. Passing remarks made about our appearance when we were very young leave their imprint, particularly the negative ones. They seem to get frozen in time along with the hurt child of that moment. In later years that child, together with the perceived flaws, becomes part of the adult's self image. Vanity usually stems from fear, fear of rejection, fear of losing our looks, fear of ourselves.

Which physical characteristic troubles you the most? Are you especially aware of it in the company of other people? If so, in what way? Be very clear about this. Explain it to yourself either in writing or talking aloud to your mirrored reflection. Don't try to rationalize why, unless it helps. Acknowledging the problem is enough.

Adrian was in his forties. By Western standards he was short. For many men this is no problem, but for Adrian it was. He constantly referred to his lack of height when he was with other people. His friends were sometimes dismayed at the constant jokes he made about it. They felt almost forced to lose sight of this fine and attractive person, because of the caricature he portrayed. 'All good things come tightly packed', he would say with a lovely grin, but his body was saying something quite different – arms tightly folded across the chest, shoulders hunched to the ears, and a defiant stance. These gestures spoke about protection.

Adrian had hoped that cracking jokes would help him to be less inhibited about his size. It hadn't worked. Finally he decided to face himself and the problem. He began to consider how minding being short affected his life, and the way he interacted with other people. 'It wasn't easy at first. I just sat down and said to myself, "Yes I mind about being short". I said it a lot of times. Then I said, "Unless I wear built-up shoes, and that I will not, there's nothing I can do about it!" Some men are aggressive or show off. I suppose that's what I was doing by cracking jokes. Being male and being short isn't easy you know, at least for me it isn't. I just left it at that. I still mind, but since then it doesn't seem to bother me – the way it did before.'

Unlike Adrian, Jenny felt unable to talk to anyone about the shape of her nose. Yet because of it she thought no one could really love her. 'I always seem to end up the victim in a relationship, and it's all because of this nose. You see I'm so grateful when someone says they like me that I let them boss me about. It's my fault really, I set it up like that.'

It transpired that even as a very small child she had been made to feel self-conscious about her nose and, indeed, it was longer than average. Her mother had laughingly referred to it when she was with her friends, no doubt as her form of protection, acknowledging what was deemed to be her offspring's flaw, before anyone else remarked upon it. At school Jenny had been teased. Had she ever thought of discussing her appearance with a counsellor? 'No, you can't go to a counsellor about your nose, not when so many people have got real problems. Besides, they'd think I was vain.'

Had she been able to talk about her nose, recognizing that it was for her a real problem, she would have saved herself much hurt. She had two alternatives; to take the plunge and have cosmetic surgery to alter the shape, or to work with a counsellor in recognizing her own worth and accepting her nose the way it was.

Sadly neither Jenny nor Adrian seemed aware of their many attractive qualities: wide smile, huge eyes, graceful walk and, most important of all, immensely likeable personalities.

Expression

When we think about appearance, expression, particularly facial expression, is often overlooked. Yet this is the key to how we respond to others, and they to us. Sometimes the nicest people forget to allow their niceness to shine through. A monk of great kindness unconsciously concealed his inner goodness by a somewhat forbidding countenance. Consequently many people meeting him for the first time were anxious and a little afraid. Finally someone pointed this out. The result was a beaming monk. Then everyone benefited from his glow, even passers-by.

Allow your positive qualities, feelings of goodwill, humour, trust, to shine through. It is guaranteed that if you feel *good* about yourself, this will project through the eyes, the smile, the greeting, the walk. Remember that your expression can also make someone else feel good about themselves. As you discover the many positive qualities you have to offer, offer them to others. Appearance is not just the nuts and bolts, it is the expression – and that can grow more beautiful with the passing of years.

Personality

The way we speak, mannerisms and bearing, are means to express the personality. They can also be guises to conceal it. For example, shyness can be expressed either as timidity or talkativeness. Disliking ourselves may be reflected as aggression or being on the defensive. Insecurity can turn into over-sensitivity, vulnerability to any remark that could be construed as rejection or a put down. A need for love, a longing to be liked, may lead us constantly to portray ourselves as a victim. Our self-esteem may be so low that we feel the only way to receive kindness is through sympathy. Hurt in the past may lead us to create a serious and somewhat unsmiling invisible circle around us. Feeling an outsider or misfit may leave us literally standing on the outside, with a message of 'fragile and lonely' written all over us. Sadly the 'I'm all right' people, being the way they are, may not respond to the message with human warmth.

'Thinking about yourself is self-centred.' Such admonishments, probably in childhood, leave one feeling guilty. We try to repress the things about ourselves that we don't like, only to find that they surface more frequently. Then even more guilt arises, because we are not supposed to think about ourselves. Thinking from the small me perspective is tunnelled, and carries with it a sense of apartness. There are them and us, and we are different. Often they seem to be against us. Each day seems a battle, as if life is not on our side. We hardly acknowledge that life breathes itself into us. 'Me' thinks I organize that too. So we get exhausted, angry, critical of ourselves, afraid and lonely. 'Maybe I won't be able to hold it all together . . . I'm a bad person . . . I must try to be more friendly.' Me is probably trying very hard, too hard.

To alleviate the sense of separation it can help to see yourself and everyone else as just life, expressions of the universe. When you pass by people clutching plastic carriers, holding briefcases, getting on bicycles, jumping off buses, or racing to school, say to yourself 'there goes life'. This perspective leads to goodwill and humour – all of us in the same up and down boat.

Courageous, honest self-awareness is not self-centred. Look at what is. Not how you were in the past, but how you are right now. Acknowledging the faults, weaknesses and difficult parts of our personality is absolutely necessary.

Awareness is the first step towards change, even transformation. We need to understand and be patient with the hurt or spoilt child within ourselves. If we do this we become more tolerant towards other people as well. Look inwards with love, not with aversion. As Louise Hay points out in her book, *You Can Heal Your Life*, '. . . criticism locks us into the pattern we are trying to change . . . Remember you have been criticising yourself for years and it hasn't worked. Try approving of yourself and see what happens.' Just one assumed flaw can distort a whole self-image. The small me in each of us wants to be approved of, liked, even perfect, but according to whose criteria? As part of the Big I we are beyond that.

Character

The *Oxford Dictionary*'s definition of the word 'character' has three parts: (1) All those qualities that make a person what he/she is . . . and different from others (2) A person's moral nature (3) Moral strength. 'In character' is that which is appropriate to a person's character; 'out of character' is that which is not appropriate. These descriptions reaffirm our independence and individuality, yet the mystery is that at the same time we are also interdependent with everything that surrounds us, everything in the cosmos. There is in truth no separation, everything is in everything! This theory is clearly explained in a beautiful book entitled *The Heart of Understanding* by Thich Nhat Hanh. Although the author is a Buddhist monk, the book is appropriate for people of any persuasion. It is recommended reading.

Defining our own character is not always easy. Most likely we have some understanding of it, but feel that others often misinterpret us. Perhaps because of a negative self-image we are projecting the wrong qualities: 'I'm not like that, he/she didn't understand', 'They think I'm a killjoy', 'People seem to back off, but I don't know why', 'People get enthusiastic then lose interest; I suppose they find me boring'.

Exercise: Assessing character

Review the perceptions you have about your character by listing the qualities you view as positive, and those you view as negative or hindrances to your own good. An assessment might go something like this:

Attributes	Hindrances
Gentle	Too apologetic. Feel everything is my fault
When it really comes to the crunch am strong underneath	Seem to be afraid of many things
Sense of humour	Being eroded by loneliness
Enthusiastic, interested in politics, people and life	Seem to talk too intensely about matters which concern me. People back off. Inflexible and mind when other people's opinions differ
A loving person	Get too attached. Love too much, or is this dependence?
Like to help people	Find it easier to be sympathetic and help those with problems. Tend to get a bit jealous of friends who are having a good time, particularly when I'm down

Look at the above example. Point one under 'attributes' is 'gentle', but this is being confused with its opposite number, 'too apologetic'. Probably this person appears gentle because they feel everything is their fault and they accept the blame for everything, even when someone bumps into them. They are setting up a situation of which others may unconciously take advantage. Next on the positive side is written 'strong underneath'. But this is being hidden by 'afraid of many things'. The word 'underneath' is the real clue. They know deep down they have real strength and courage, particularly when it comes to a demanding situation. Unconsciously they may think that apology and being afraid are aspects that others will respond to, rather better than strength with gentleness. They need to remind themselves that with the former they are not their own person; with the latter they are.

Decide whether *your* assessment is fair, or whether it is dominated by negative beliefs. If it is the latter, the next step is to consider how to redress the balance. Sit quietly and feel the positive qualities. Meditate on them. Repeat to yourself for example 'gentle and strong', 'strong and gentle'. Feel the words, and how they pervade your being, for they are you. Again, blaming yourself for something that is not your responsibility is to undervalue yourself. It is also a form of patronage towards other people and leads you to project an untrue image. Take the last item on the list, 'like to help people' opposed by 'easier to be sympathetic to those with problems. Resent others' good fortune if I am having a bad time.' Don't be hard on yourself for this honesty. It is entirely human. However resentment has to go, or it will manifest in some form or other.

It may help to see the fortunate person as just *life*, rather than a particular friend. For example, **A** has just joined up with a partner. **B** is still longing for that to happen. Hearing the good news of **A** makes **B** even more lonely – understandable. **B** feels envious. Envy or resentment won't hurt **A**, but it will hurt **B**. Each of us has to find a way to dissolve envy or jealousy. Sometimes just acknowledging the jealousy and the pain it brings, does the trick. 'Yes I am envious of his/her good luck, it makes me feel awful, even more hollow, even more alone, in fact it physically hurts.' Keep saying it until it brings a rueful smile. With that, envy transfers to the gentler state of wistfulness.

C and **D** are out of work. They are having a difficult time, but their companionship keeps them going. Fortune smiles on **C**, who is offered a great job. **D** hears the news and inwardly begins to panic. Thoughts of wishing it had happened to him, and emotions of fear and loneliness arise spontaneously as a result of **C**'s good fortune. **D** need not feel guilty at not rejoicing; but in order that the troubling emotions don't build up, **D** needs to sit in the middle of the pain and fear without judgement or repression. Staring the negative thoughts and emotions in the face means they will eventually dissolve.

Both B and D then, the ones without the good news, need to think positively about their own future. 'Something good is going to happen to me very soon, I know it, I feel it, I deserve it.'

Looking at our characteristics and considering how we can overcome the difficult parts helps us to a truer and more positive image of ourselves. In this way the rest of the previous picture would be adjusted to read as a statement of positive intention:

Attributes	Intention	Hindrances
Sense of humour	Loneliness doesn't alter funny side of life. Must be careful to remember this. Watch out about sad facial expression, becoming too serious	Being eroded by loneliness
Enthusiastic, interested in politics, people and life	Now I must be more aware and pull back if getting too intense. Must allow others to have their views, and learn to listen without interrupting. Open the heart	Talk too intensely about matters of concern. Inflexible and mind when other people's opinions differ
A loving person	There, I have said it. Being attached is not love. So I have to 'let go', step back. Not easy, but I'll work on it! Must remember I'm a whole, brave and independent person	Get too attached. Love too much, but in my heart I know this is dependency

Perceptions of Yourself 23

If you discover you are projecting an unbalanced picture because of the negative beliefs you have about yourself, start to look after yourself immediately by adjusting the image.

A deep sense of loneliness can arise from thinking it is impossible or too late to change. It is never impossible or too late. Everything is changing all the time. Neither are we helpless victims of our thoughts, they choosing us rather than we choosing them. 'My thoughts seem to take over. I get carried along with them.' We are responsible for what we think, and can change our thought patterns whenever we wish. We have the power to change the direction of our thoughts at any time. That is freedom. It may take a few weeks of determined effort to eradicate the old way of thinking, but if you persevere it will happen, and it will work. This does not mean we must retreat from pain. On the contrary the only way to overcome mental pain of any kind and in certain instances physical pain, is to go right into it. Stay with it until it dissolves of its own accord.

THE ESSENCE

We are not here to be like someone else. We are here to be ourselves. To be our own person, and our own body. Let go, allow everything to be or do itself, then you will be yourself.

Each person's true nature, the inner essence, is profound and deeply private. If we are still, we can hear it within the silence. It is innocence, it is pure, empty, open to everything; it is awareness, true hearing, it is joy and love. It is the ageless child. That which speaks through the heart, the eyes, the smile, the caring, concern, laughter, the generosity, the greeting. This child cannot permeate our whole being unless we understand that we, all of us, are worthy of the child. For it is I.

CHAPTER THREE

Relating to Others

OUR 'OTHER FAMILY'

Each of us has two families. The conventional one resulting
from blood ties, marriage, country or creed, and for want of
a better word that 'other family' which may have no connection with these ties. Strangely, it is rare to encounter our other
family. Some of us never do. Why? Is it because we are
in the wrong job, environment, or because of limiting circumstances? Is it because we are afraid of loneliness and stick
with the first people who come along, or because all along the
line our opinions, prejudices and preconceptions block the
natural flow of change? Perhaps none of these reasons is a
contributory factor. The truth is that all over the world there
are your and my family, yet for some unaccountable reason
so often we are washed up on different shores.

Reflecting upon the whereabouts of our other family and
taking practical steps that might lead us to them poses no
threat to those close to us. A dearly loved partner or friend
may not be a member of that other family. This in no way
implies they are second best or not really right for us, for
there is no competition or measurement. One story has
nothing to do with the other. Nor is it about love in the
conventional sense, simply another story connected with
each of our lives.

Both sides know instinctively when they meet someone
from the other family. The link is an immediate empathy
and awareness of those deep intangible qualities which can
only be sensed, never extracted by words. Vitality fills our
being. Conversation is easy; no compromise is required;

we have no need to try too hard. Our encounter may only be as ships passing in the night but, at one with each other, we part nourished.

Search for your other family – you may meet up, you may not. Perhaps the time and conditions are not appropriate. Never give up on the belief that members of your other family are just around the corner. Positive thinking is a powerful force to precipitate such a meeting. Physical or artistic activities, study, specialized interests, exploring spiritual inclinations, gardening, cooking, making things, listening to music, books, nature, walking, lying on the back doing absolutely nothing – enjoying those interests and individual things which particularly open our hearts, our heads and our thinking unite us to both our families.

COMPROMISE

The *Oxford Dictionary* describes compromise as 'making a settlement by each side giving up part of its demands . . . something that is half way between opposite opinions or course of actions'.

In the best sense of the word, compromise is a putting aside of some of the small me, putting aside some of our 'wants' – not needs, but 'wants'. Each of us has to compromise in some way or another, because nothing remains the same for ever. Change is taking place from moment to moment. If we compromise with the wholehearted intention of making something work, relationships and friendships can be cemented in quite unexpected ways. If the same sincere intention is applied to our working lives, particularly with reference to difficult colleagues, life can become more relaxed.

Within ourselves we may need to compromise in order that we can accept ourselves as we are right now. If the challenge of compromise is met, we begin to explore a magical art, the art of improvisation. Improvisation is a challenge to the imagination, one that stretches our potential to be inventive and resourceful. Being ready and able to improvise in all situations is a valuable skill that will stand us in good stead throughout life.

Compromise is only dangerous when it comes about

through fear, through not being able to face up to the truth, done for approval, for selfish gain or as an easy option. Compromising for any of these reasons compromises our true nature, our integrity and our individuality. We hand over our power to someone else and expose ourselves to danger.

EXPECTATIONS

Expectation, like everything else in life, has both a positive and a negative side. It can spur us on to greater fulfilment, to stretch ourselves, or to kick serious negative habits. In such instances we appreciate and respond to expectation as a force to help us move forward. But expectation of the small me kind is weakening, destructive and invariably leads to disappointment. We invest our ideals in other people, particularly in relationships, and then feel personally abused when these ideals cannot be met.

The root from which this kind of expectation stems is insecurity. Feeling unable to stand foursquare without another's support, we often in a somewhat self-righteous manner transfer our own inadequacies and weaknesses on to the other person, and are consequently devastated when things go wrong. Small me expectation, particularly in a relationship, can lead to harmful dependency, hurt, resentment, loneliness and even paranoia.

Naturally there is disappointment if our hopes about someone else are dashed. However this need not be a cause for psychological wounds. We are safe so long as that disappointment is not interpreted as personal rejection or a deliberate affront and rather, with wisdom, see and understand it as the other person's problem. This is not to suggest accepting or condoning wrong behaviour. We may need to extricate ourselves from someone's negative orbit. When this has to happen, hang on to your bootstraps and remind yourself that you are looking after the welfare of both parties, that your decision is wise and brave.

People change, some can be relied upon, others not, but ultimately the most reliable friend has to be ourselves. If we understand this and treat ourselves accordingly, we also can be 'best friends' for other people.

Use the experience of loneliness as a teacher to help dissolve negative egocentric expectation. When we have learnt to be at peace with our own company, we begin to enjoy life as independent people – fully enjoying and interacting with others but equally comfortable alone.

FRIENDSHIP

Most of us resist putting ourselves aside in order to get to know and understand another person. We greet people, particularly those close to us, with yesterday's eyes and yesterday's memories. The great teacher Krishnamurti, frequently drew his audience's attention to this fact when he spoke. In his book *The First and Last Freedom* he wrote:

> You see a lovely sunset, a beautiful tree in a field. When you first look at it, you enjoy it completely, wholly; but you go back to it with the desire to enjoy it again. What happens when you go back with the desire to enjoy it? There is no enjoyment because it is the memory of yesterday's sunset making you return . . . Yesterday there was no memory only a spontaneous appreciation, a direct response . . . This is memory intervening between you and the sunset . . . Again, you have a friend who said something to you yesterday, an insult or compliment, and you retain the memory: with that memory you meet your friend today. You do not really meet your friend – you carry with you the memory of yesterday which intervenes.

Likewise, Thich Nhat Hanh in *The Heart of Understanding* writes: 'A husband and wife who wish to understand each other have to be in the skin of their partner in order to feel, otherwise they cannot really understand . . . You cannot love someone if you do not understand him or her. If you don't understand and you love, that is not love; it is something else.'

First Impressions

We need to be cautious of making hasty judgements and being dismissive about people. 'They are not on my wavelength', 'We have nothing in common', 'She looks unfriendly',

'He's a smart alec', 'She's got lots of friends, she won't want to get to know me', 'He looks really boring; that's the last thing I want'.

Why do we not allow time before jumping to conclusions? Perhaps we all feel victims of time. The mind's appreciation of time, however, is relative. A moment can seem instantaneous or eternal. To prevent hasty judgements, free yourself from time. Put yourself aside and observe the scene from a neutral place. Let the ears hear, the eyes see and an awakened mind do the rest. As all this is happening, be conscious of your breath, breathing in, breathing out. Following the breath helps to stabilize and slow everything down. Greet both new and familiar people with an open mind and generous heart as if for the first time. We are not here to judge but to be ourselves. Devote full moment by moment attention to whomever you are with. Total attention creates a stillness within, a space free of opinionated internal chatter. Full attention can be difficult to sustain at first, but with practice and patience it is definitely a skill which can be acquired. When the monkey mind darts about in all directions, gently bring it back to the object of your attention. Once the art of total attention is mastered, interaction becomes easy. Goodwill and confidence are generated. You feel in control, you have let go of time to give full attention to the other person.

The experience of loneliness used positively teaches us to be at peace with our own company. This also helps us to make wise choices in friendship when the opportunity arises. Never be pressurized into having to make friends by some well-meaning person who has introduced you to a number of people because they know you are lonely. Take your time. Joining the wrong party can be far more lonely than being alone.

'Tough Love' in Friendship

Friendship occasionally requires what is known in self-help groups as 'tough love'. Tough love means having the courage and concern to point out something disagreeable that a friend may not wish to hear.

Mary recalled a period of her life when she moved from one destructive relationship to another. 'I was out of control, passions and fear took over. Looking back I see it as an illness, a breakdown of rationality. I was unaware of what it was doing to my family or me. I remember towards the end of the whole sorry business removing a leaf from the car windscreen. It was a gorgeous golden brown colour. Suddenly I realized it was autumn – my favourite season. I hadn't even noticed it. Whatever happened to summer? I wondered.'

'Didn't anyone point out the damage you were doing to yourself, to your family?'

'Not really, friends were wonderfully kind and listened endlessly to my problems. In a way I wish they had been less understanding. You know, really spelt it out loud and clear. But then again maybe I wouldn't have taken any notice. Probably not for me, but for the family *maybe*. Even then they were the most precious.'

Mary's friend was asked why she had not been tough. 'She wouldn't have listened.' Perhaps not, but rather than the kindly ear of friendship, it might have been more compassionate to mete out 'tough love', confronting her with the reality of the situation. If it didn't work, it didn't. The fifty per cent chance that it might work is always worth the effort.

Friendship is appreciating the concerns of others, even when there is something we don't want to hear. It is sharing the sorrows and celebrating the joys. It is allowing the other person to have 'off' days without a sense of rejection. Being open, explaining situations clearly so that everyone knows where they stand. Friendship is loyalty, support, sensitivity, and *never* playing games.

If for the time being you are somewhat friendless, remember that there are many other people all over the world in the same position, all lovable people, just as you are. Do not allow the present experience of loneliness to deplete your spirit. An air of sorrow or depression casts a shadow that other people pick up and back away from. Hang on with courage, beam out love to yourself and others, both those you know and those you don't know. You will not be lonely for long.

LONERS

Some of us are born 'loners', but such aloneness need not be confused with loneliness. Loners are not necessarily friendless. On the contrary, there are loners who have an embarrassment of close friends and acquaintances. Yet they remain aloof, within their own space. Those who recognize this part of their nature enjoy company, but the jewel in their crown is solitude.

Obviously, loners find it difficult to be 'joiners'. Many people who suffer from loneliness are to some extent by nature loners. The mistake is in not recognizing this and coming to terms with it. Confused loners keep endeavouring to become joiners. They join groups, activities, clubs, go on outings. When they start to feel uneasy they put it down to being a complicated person, a misfit, not being liked. At school the child loner is looked upon with uncertainty by teachers and students. In our society group pressure begins at an early age. The conventional social image of a successful person includes being surrounded by bright people. So confused loners either retreat into their shells, or compromise their nature by joining without any sense of fitting in or belonging.

Andrew spoke of his experience as a loner. 'I was born a loner. As a child I had many friends whom I loved, yet there was an apartness. School outings and camps were a real strain. I so wished I could be a joiner. This wishing began to emerge as an inner loneliness, which resulted in many mistakes in later life. When at last I recognized and accepted how I am, everything began to fall into place. I must confess, though, there is still a wistfulness about not being a "joiner". I find even talking to the nicest people gets tiring after a time. My friends are used to me now. When I say, "Right, I'm off", no one bothers. They used to say "Oh you're not going yet, it's too early", and that sort of thing.'

'Are you lonely?'

Andrew took a long time to consider the question. 'Yes, in a way, but gently so.'

CHAPTER FOUR

The Art of Interaction

Interaction and communication are an art rather than something that just happens when people get together. Each of us possesses the qualities to refine the way we communicate so that it becomes an art. The question is, are we aware of these qualities? They can be polished up until they shine, or sadly neglected. If the latter, everyone misses out. Skilful communication demonstrates a respect for ourselves and the rest of life. The most important ingredients for successful interaction are:

> Sensitivity, sincerity and awareness:
> Kindness, generosity, being able to give full attention to whoever we are with
> Being encouraging and positive
> Being able to put people at their ease, making them feel special and interesting
> Meeting with an open and generous heart
> Letting go of time, so that even five minutes to spare is given with the impression that time is of no consequence
> Knowing when to stop talking
> Being conscious of how to express goodwill and interest through facial expression, posture and gesture
> Keeping a sense of humour, smiling inside as well as outside

We have the potential to use all these qualities. Check the list to see whether they are being developed to the full in you.

When we interact with other people, it is important not to appear overwhelmingly negative, even if at times we feel depleted and lacking in confidence and self-esteem. Communicate with an open and generous heart to each and everyone.

Occasionally the goodwill you offer may be rejected or ignored. If this ever happens, be sure not to let it make you return to your shell. The problem lies with the other person not you. It is their loss.

Warmth and kindness are never wasted; they are enriching in the most unexpected ways.

GREETING AND PARTING

How we greet can colour the rest of the meeting. How we part can affect the rest of the day. A depressed or unsure greeting means immediately handing over your power to someone else. The surliest character will be disarmed by a warm sincere greeting.

To ensure a successful meeting, be positive from the outset even if you are filled with dread. Have the sincere intent to make the encounter a good experience. 'This is going to be all right, in fact far better than just all right.' Greet with an expression and gestures that speak of welcome and friendship – a kiss, handshake, nod, or expansive embrace. Whatever the gesture, mean it. Make direct eye contact and beam out a smile. The Indian form of greeting and parting, hands together in prayer position and a small bow of the head, is an attractive gesture which speaks of respect and giving up a small part of oneself. It also dispenses with the need to select who you embrace or shake hands with. Well, here we are in the ungainly West, with our own customs and gestures, so we might as well use them as gracefully as we can.

Partings require similar attention. The perfunctory peck on the cheek, the limp embrace or the wave over the shoulder as you dash for the bus can leave a somewhat vacant conclusion rather than a friendly full stop.

If we lack confidence or are depressed it can be difficult to make direct eye contact and smile spontaneously. Focusing on the breath helps. Just before the moment of greeting take in a long slow breath. With the exhalation visualize all your heaviness of heart being released into the air. Let go. Say to yourself, 'Open the heart'. Surrender to the moment and there will be no problem. The ageless child within you is freed to smile through the eyes.

SMILING

Why in the Western world does so little spontaneous, every-day smiling go on? Are shyness or fear of rebuff the main culprits? Has it something to do with climatic conditions? People are reflections of their landscape. Here a lot more smiling goes on when the sun is out. In public places we walk past each other, sit opposite each other or queue behind each other with anxious or forbidding countenances. Yet when we do pluck up courage to smile at someone, their face is transformed as they return the smile. Again the ageless child is freed. Any negative opinions that we might have conjured up about a total stranger go out with the bathwater. One smile has bonded two people.

Smiling is universally healing. Good things happen to the body as a result of smiling. Whether alone or with others, cultivate a tiny smile as part of your natural expression.

LISTENING

The jewel in the crown of communication is the art of listening. Everyone likes to be in the company of a person who really hears what they have to say. A good listener is always appreciated and popular. A good listener becomes a 'hearer', someone who is an active participant, giving full attention moment by moment to whomever they are with. Total attention cannot be stressed enough. It is the key to success. The art of hearing requires practice. Krishnamurti spoke of total attention:

> I do not know if you have ever noticed that when you give total attention, there is complete silence. And in that attention there is no frontier, there is no centre as the 'me' who is aware of atten-tion . . . Silence and spaciousness go together. The immensity of silence is the immensity of mind in which the centre does not exist.

He also spoke on the art of listening:

> Most of us listen through a screen of prejudice. Either we are expecting a definite solution to our problems, or we are not

aware of the innumerable prejudices which prevent us from really hearing what another says, or we are not sufficiently interested or concentrated to listen at all. To listen truly is to listen without strain, without struggle, without the effort of hearing . . . So, if I may suggest, it will be good if we can listen without making the effort to listen, without accepting or rejecting; if we can listen without erecting a barrier of defence, or trying too eagerly to grasp what is being said. There must be a certain tension, like that of the violin string.

To be a good hearer you have to let go of time, so that there is all the time in the world to hear what is being said at that moment. Allow the words to seek the ears rather than the other way about. Interrupt only when instinct prompts. Pauses and moments of silence are all right.

The art of hearing sounds easy, but if small me gets in the way it is so difficult. If two impulsive people get together, both dying to recount their experiences, the result is a relentless tennis match, either side whamming home, hardly allowing each other to finish their sentence. Perhaps someone tells us their problems but we keep interrupting with advice or likening it to a personal experience. Or someone is holding forth with views diametrically opposed to ours. Rather than let them get things off their chest, we redirect the conversation. We don't have to agree, but at least we can be objective and hear them out. If we are shy maybe we ask a lot of questions about the other person to divert attention from ourselves. Before they have had time to reply to the first question, we launch into the next question. It becomes rather like an interrogation. Despite our interested intent posture we are not listening and the other person knows. They recognize that 'glazed eye' look, and all the 'mmm'ing' and nodding that is going on. They know we have not heard a word and retreat mortified.

Learn the art of being able to shift a boring conversation into a new direction without offence. Endless sagas can be relieved by keeping a sense of humour if the whole thing gets too much. Develop the art of making a graceful exit whilst at the same time leaving the other person intact.

Practice and attention make us good hearers.

THE VOICE

Your voice has an effect on people. To know how you sound, listen to yourself on tape. Your voice is your instrument. It can be adjusted. Each voice reveals far more than most of us realize. The telephone rings, we answer. One 'hullo' can paint a whole picture. The caller responds accordingly. A dejected 'hullo' might solicit a concerned response or make the other person wish they hadn't called. A friendly 'hullo' will set the conversation off to a good start, even if subsequently it focuses on problems or sorrows. The voice can sound tired, sad, garrulous, gossipy and spiteful, too intense, over excited, pathetically weak. Alternatively it can sound welcoming, gentle, serious, serene or bubbly. It can be lowered, raised, speeded up, slowed down. Most of us will have encountered the bureaucratic power-game telephone voice. The voice that tells you it belongs to an extremely busy person.

Your voice is your instrument; you have it in your power to use it how you choose. The tone you use can make or mar someone else's day.

CONVERSATION

The art of conversation consists of stimulating interest and drawing people out. It requires:

Sensitivity and sincerity

Being truly interested in what someone else has to say

Being able to talk with animation, and knowing when to stop

Not going on and on about oneself, unless of course there is an invitation to do so and, even then, with moderation

Being able to redirect negative conversation or gossip in a positive direction

Not speaking too quickly, too loudly, too softly, slowly or monotonously

Not interrupting, chipping in before the other person has had time to finish – interruption is often the result of being ill at ease or shy

Keeping a sense of humour when the conversation goes
  seriously wrong
Holding the listener's interest by the use of word, gesture
  and expression – our brushes and paint that colour any
  subject.

We may be out of practice both at conversing and entertaining
if a period of isolation and loneliness has meant leading a
somewhat hermit-like life. Suddenly the situation changes and
there is the opportunity to do both. We lose our nerve or feel
the whole thing is too much effort. If this happens, do not fall
into the trap of retreating. The effort has to be made. The
familiar state, even if it feels safer, is a negative one. We are
here not only for ourselves but to give support to other people
whenever the need arises.

Home may have become your private island, a refuge from
hurt. It is understandable if the idea of suddenly being able
to invite someone home for a meal, and having them there for
a number of hours, seems alarming. This is only because you
are out of practice. Once you determine to offer hospitality,
do it with your whole heart. Perhaps begin by inviting
someone for a drink, coffee, for a specific time, explaining
that later you have to be elsewhere. Gradually build up your
confidence so that you begin to enjoy entertaining again. If
at first you prefer to socialize outside the home base, invite
someone for a walk – conversation flows easily with the activity of walking – or arrange to meet somewhere congenial
and relaxed, where you can hear yourselves speak. A place
where you can spend time, but perhaps not too much money.

BODY LANGUAGE

The ways we stand, walk, wait, sit, greet, turn our heads, are
weather vanes to how we feel. Notice how your body reacts
when you are afraid, defensive, unhappy or depressed. The
shoulders hunch up, the head droops, the back sags, arms are
crossed over so that the chest closes in. Unconsciously we
have shrunk. This posture blocks the flow of energy that

circulates around the body and compounds the stress. Our body is saying, 'Keep away, I'm down, I'm not worthy of being noticed, no one likes me'. And negative posture only deepens the depression. Despite your distress, let go. Make yet another courageous effort. Let the body open outwards and upwards. Allow the body to celebrate life rather than mourn it. Doing this alleviates inner pain. You are in control, rather than being the hapless victim of your thoughts or situation.

Gestures which speak of respect, enthusiasm and caring concern are ours to give freely. Our body language affects other people. There is much that is grey and sad within this world. We have it in our power just by the way we express and deport ourselves to contribute to that greyness or, despite our own problems, make a generous effort to offset it.

Step outside yourself occasionally to see what your body is doing. The complexities of the mind muddle the body. Let go and allow the body to do itself. It will, with grace and ease.

Once the art of communication is mastered every encounter takes on a richer meaning. Give full attention to each and everyone. Practise with the help of these suggestions. If you feel you have lost your confidence, take off on a course designed to pitch you outwards. Don't forget the smile.

CHAPTER FIVE

Strategies for Transforming Loneliness

The two essential ingredients for transforming loneliness are positive thinking and a genuine love and acceptance of yourself as you are right now. So many problems and illnesses arise through constantly criticizing and berating ourselves. Most of us are doing our very best, and if we could be different at this moment, we would be. This philosophy is beautifully stated in Louise Hay's book *You Can Heal Your Life*, a practical and helpful guide to self-acceptance and positive thinking. Psychology and self-help sections in bookshops display many good books on positive thinking and related subjects; it is worth browsing through them.

Loneliness can cause a state of inner poverty because of the need to love and be loved. Everyone in the world needs and deserves love. We do not have to earn love. We just need to realize and trust the fact that absolute love surrounds us all the time. That same boundless love is our wealth to give out, and it is independent of the whims, affections, responses or behaviour of others. A willingness to change, to discard old negative thinking patterns, to improvise in a difficult situation and to laugh at ourselves are the other qualities to develop.

Since loneliness is unlikely to disappear overnight we might as well make use of the experience. Flowers grow with the nourishment of composted rubbish; so can we. You may be saying, 'Yes, this sounds fine, but the spark has gone. I'm too tired, too many knocks.' The spark never goes. It may be flickering but, given a chance, it is as bubbly as you when you were at playschool.

Never give up. Fairy stories are not to be disparaged – they can and do happen, sometimes in the most unexpected manner. The power of positive thinking has its own mysterious force.

Shortly before his death, Joseph Campbell, the American anthropologist, and a man of great insight, was interviewed on television. He was asked to give one piece of advice to young people. Smiling broadly and without a moment's hesitation he said, 'Follow your own bliss . . . go ahead and do it'. Brilliant advice for any age. Suggestions to liberate the spirit often evoke resistance: 'Oh well, that's OK for someone without responsibilities . . . in privileged circumstances . . . if I were younger.' 'Yes, but it's not as easy as that.' Following your bliss means following your heart. It could involve dramatic change, or it could mean no upheaval, just becoming involved with something simple, something you've always wanted to have a go at but never got round to doing. (Chapter 6 looks at this in more depth.)

APPRECIATING SILENCE

The record player, radio and television are marvellous companions if we live alone but there is the danger of becoming too dependent on them and using them to fill voids.

Campbell talked about tuning into the creative part of ourselves and hearing what it has to say. 'Listening' and 'hearing' can be very different. Hearing is allowing the hearing consciousness to be used to its full capacity. This means not being afraid of either inner or outer silence. Growing to appreciate silence is a huge step towards transforming loneliness. Silence can then be enjoyed rather than denied.

Hearing and silence go hand in hand. Hearing is the only way to appreciate silence, the thunderous roar of silence. One way to begin to train the ear is by repeatedly giving your full attention to music, hearing all the different instruments, harmonies, words, rhythms. At first this may require an effort, but when mastered the music is truly heard so that the hearer and sound become one. Closed eyes help. Let the sound seek the ear rather than the other way about. If you try this the ears can feel literally as if they are opening out.

Hearing the music of daily life is another way to train the ear. Again, let the sound seek the ear – the song of the bird, the sound of raindrops, the breath, the wind. Even aggressive man-made sounds take on a new quality if they are heard as sound rather than being identified with the object that causes them. Of course sound can be desperately unsettling and lonely – the blaring record player, the all-night party – then the only solution is a pair of wax earplugs.

Begin to introduce times of silence into the day. Basic meditation practice or just sitting quietly are the best ways to grow accustomed to silence. It is of great benefit to health and well-being to sit quietly for at least ten minutes twice a day.

Should you be interested in exploring meditation, it is wise to join a group with a teacher who is skilled in its basic practice. Basic meditation is a way to let go of everything and to sit peacefully with the moment. Practising meditation under the guidance of a teacher does not necessarily mean having to accept a particular system of religious thought. (For information on meditation and retreat centres *see* 'Further Reading'.)

The exercise below gives a few guidelines to start you off. The instructions are for sitting but are equally suitable if you prefer to lie on your back.

Exercise: Resting the body and mind

Sit on a chair, or on the floor, in a cross-legged position or on your heels with feet tucked under you. The important thing is to keep the back in an upright position. The back of the head pushes up towards the ceiling, the chin is tucked in and the ears are in line with the shoulders. Fold your hands peacefully in your lap or let them rest on the knees. Close or half close the eyes. Breathe in and out slowly and deeply. Let any tiredness, tenseness, anxiety, sorrow, confusion just drain away through the fingertips, through the feet, the toes, the back, through the chest, the cheeks, through the skull. Let it all go as you breathe in and out. Let the chair or floor support your weight.

Simply sit in the moment breathing in and out, in and out. For these few moments you don't have to do anything, be anything or achieve anything. You are supported by the air, the light, the space, the planet, the universe. Release any tension that has built up in the body. Soften the facial muscles, the cheeks, the mouth. Relax the skull, imagine the brain having room to stretch out and rest in stillness. Release any tension in the back of the head and neck. Let go. Put your hand gently at the base of the throat and allow the whole of the upper chest to soften. Let go of time; there is no time, there is only now.

Feel a sense of love for the body which is so loyal. Rest the hands and fingers which work so hard, rest the spinal column which supports the frame. Let go of any tension in the legs and feet. If thoughts crowd in let them pass as clouds over your sky. Take no notice of interruptions from the small me mind. At this moment you are one with the Big I mind. Hear the silence and allow life to flow through the body. Open your heart to absolute goodness, in you and around you. Feel that you are breathing in peace, and breathing out peace. Rest in the space of silence. Rest in the space of stillness.

These quiet periods are havens from the chaos of the outside world. Try introducing a few minutes of silence into your daily activities as well. No background sounds, and if possible, no internal chatter. Just pay full attention to whatever you are doing – dressing, washing up – hear the sounds that are caused by the actions, and the spaces of silence in between. Active silence, however short, brings a sense of inner order, a feeling of being grounded.

OTHER STRATEGIES

Remind yourself each day that the condition of inner loneliness is not going to last and that social loneliness (*see* Chapter 11) is a common problem almost entirely due to sociological factors.

If lonely because of living alone, are there any pluses to compensate for the minuses? Does the current situation bring with it a certain amount of freedom such as being accountable only to yourself, the freedom to choose the daily routine and change it whenever?

Never feel guilty about enjoying aspects of being alone. Common reactions from people who are lonely can be 'Living alone makes for a selfish person'. The answer is, 'Only if you choose to let it be so.' 'I feel so selfish doing all this only for me.' Answer: 'Why? It would be far more selfish if you neglected yourself, and others had to pick up the pieces.' 'I never bother to cook for myself, it's not worth it.' Answer: 'Since we are primarily here to learn for the sake of ourselves, rather than for the sake of others, is this not somewhat presumptuous? Only the small me thinks on these lines, not the mind of the Big I.'

Surrounded by family or friends yet inwardly lonely? This may mean you need more time to be alone and do things by yourself. A feeling of being hemmed in can cause loneliness. Don't be put off if others feel threatened by your need for occasional privacy or outings on your own. Explain the reasons in a way that leaves others feeling secure rather than rejected. What is right for you will in the long term be right for those close to you. Stephanie Dowricke's book *Balancing Closeness and Independence* is recommended.

If the sense of inner loneliness is acute never feel you have to work through this condition on your own. (*See also* Chapter 7, Coping with Acute Loneliness.)

PITFALLS

Being lonely is demoralizing. It can lead one to feel a constant victim, a victim of other people's indifference or unkindness, a victim of society, of life. Though understandable, this is a downward spiral and must stop. Seeing ourselves as the victim of any situation means we are not our own person and have handed over our power (a point stressed in Louise Hay's *You Can Heal Your Life*). Each of us is responsible for what we think; we choose our thoughts and they colour the events that take place in our lives. The good thing is that negative thought patterns can be changed. (Chapter 7 suggests ways to do this.) Once we are aware that we see ourselves as a victim we no longer have the excuse to be one.

Another pitfall, having been hurt by loneliness, is to lose trust in other people. Here there is a danger of beginning to live selfishly; it all becomes too much effort. To overcome this requires a positive attitude and a physical determination to get going with an open heart.

THE HOME BASE

Home, however modest, is our refuge from the outside world. It needs to be as beautiful as we can make it. Inexpensive touches can transform even the dingiest of rooms. A bright bedcover or tablecloth, gentle lighting rather than a stark overhead bulb, a pot of flowers, or cheerful plants. Home has to be friendly. Taking a bath by candlelight can be very peaceful.

Our objects are friends. Everything has its own quality if there is respect for both place and object. We are all connected with the objects that surround us. Consider the story of a metal chair with a cotton seat. The metal started life as particles of matter in the universe, so did we. The cotton seat once grew proudly in the earth where the sun and rain nourished it, as it does us. Someone picked the cotton, manufactured the metal and put the chair together. The universe is in both ourselves and the chair.

GOING OUT

Make a list of all the things you want to do, but find difficult to do alone: going on holiday, going out for a meal, to the cinema, on a long walk or an expedition to the sea. On a good day pick one of these things to do alone. Start with the least demanding situation. Don't be intimidated because you seem to be the only person on your own; don't accept second best – if you go out for a meal and don't like the table, ask for another. It takes courage at first, but it is part of the course. Recognizing self-worth is essential for enjoying outings alone. If it is a strain at first, it won't be for long. An open face, an open smile and confident body posture can disarm even the most surly of characters (see Chapter 4).

Doing things alone may not be as much fun as being with a friend, but it is better than being stuck with the wrong one. It can be quite liberating to observe couples who seem to have little to say to one another. You can sigh with relief because now you have the confidence to step out alone and enjoy life.

CHAPTER SIX

Creating a Daily Structure

RITUAL

Everyone has an instinctive if unconscious need for some kind of ritual in their life, whether as a private experience or as part of a community. In Northern Europe and particularly the UK there is a lack of opportunity to take part in public ritual. This is sad, because such events can forge a bond, a sense of belonging, a connection with the earth and heavens.

Public ritual or ceremony is performed with the purpose of bringing people together to revere, thank or celebrate. The anthropologist, Joseph Campbell, said of ritual, 'It helps to pitch us out'. Novalis, an eighteenth-century German poet, wrote, 'The secret of the soul is there where the outer and inner worlds meet'.

Though the opportunities to participate and enjoy communal ritual may be scarce, what we can and often unconsciously do is create our own. Seemingly mundane actions and routine habits can become ceremonies and celebrations of life, or the cosmos, or nature, or God – whatever the heart reveres and inclines towards.

Creating our own ritual in daily life helps the inner and outer worlds to meet. We reconnect with the awe, the wonder of the spontaneous and ageless child. A sense of awe may help to cut our problems down to size. Homemade ritual provides us with a set of self-made rules, an order to sustain us through the good and bad times. Ritual helps us not to wobble. Ritual places us on the earth firmly as a participator rather than just a consumer.

Specific daily actions can become our private ritual. As such each action has quality and significance. When it comes to creating our own ritual, living alone can be an advantage. Personal ritual can be a deeply private experience. Barry, aged forty-seven, lived in a home for chronically ill people. Great emphasis was placed by the home on the residents attending church services. Barry refused. 'Are you religious?' 'Yeah, but only in the privacy of my room!'

The way we structure each day is very important. The framework we build can alleviate the experience of loneliness, perhaps even transform it.

A POSITIVE START TO THE DAY

The first few moments of wakening can influence the rest of the day. A few moments' reflection before jumping or crawling out of bed is a positive beginning.

Themes for reflection

The miracle of darkness turning into light
Gratitude for a new day
The privilege of human life
The Big I – intelligence
Observe and feel the stillness of the objects in your room
Listen to the life sounds
Welcome any challenges and learning opportunities the
  day may provide
Decide to flow with the happenings of the day, to be
  with what is, rather than what should be
At this point smile; say out loud to yourself that the
  day is going to be a great day because you wish to
  make it so
Visualize this globe as a fragile marble amongst
  countless other marbles floating in the blackness of
  the cosmos; none of these planets knows each other
Reflect upon your five-billion-strong family as well as
  the animal, insect, bird and vegetation families, all of
  us being supported by one and the same thing – the
  breath of life

Remind yourself there is an opportunity behind every
   problem; perhaps at present we are not evolved
   enough to see beyond the immediate picture, but one
   day we will be
Hold yourself and others with love; the love you give
   yourself will determine your response to the day and
   to other people
Wish yourself well; wish others well, particularly those
   who are lonely
Transcend barriers in the mind which limit us to
   experience life with yesterday's memories or
   tomorrow's hopes; freedom is in the now
Today the sky is the limit – say it – mean it – feel it.

An everyday routine is a settled way of behaving and as such
the safety net to help us cope with the events and pressures
of a day so long as we are fully aware of our actions and
intent. A seemingly ordinary routine can change to become
the ritual of the extraordinary. All life can be seen as ordinary
or all life can be understood as extraordinary – only aeons of
conditioning have taught us to view it otherwise.

GETTING GOING

Full attention to whatever you are doing is a password for
balancing the body and mind. Be aware if you jump out of
bed in a hurry. Be aware of the hurry in your actions. Rising
with a heavy heart feeling there is little to look forward to?
Stop for a moment, shut your eyes and note the feeling of a
heavy heart. Then pull yourself up. Be positive. Look forward
to something immediate – a hot drink, going out to get a
paper, listening to a favourite radio programme, buying some
flowers for your place, eating something tasty, going for a
walk. Bowing is a positive action to begin each day with, a
movement that speaks of letting go of the small me. Bow to
whatever your heart inclines to. Make one corner of the room
a peace zone, a non-negative corner, a place to be still in, a
place to bow from. Flowers, a candle or incense will help
create a positive peaceful space. Interestingly, plants seem to
last longer in peace zones.

As you wash be aware of the sensation as water and skin meet. The miraculous availability of water is something we in the West take for granted. As the kettle boils cast a thought to the energy boiling the water, the warmth you will receive from a hot drink.

Programme yourself with a sense of inner order by leaving your place tidy before going out. Do you prefer to leave everything in chaos? Chaos is fine if it is a deliberate choice and truly makes life easier or more fun. It is essential to be honest about this because chaos can often be caused by a lack of self-discipline, a lack of self-worth, or as a political, social or environmental protest. For these reasons chaos ends up as self-punishment. Generally speaking loneliness is relieved by order. Returning home to a mess can feel unfriendly.

Throughout the day whenever things get difficult reconnect with the body. Pay total attention to whatever you do – walking up and down stairs, eating, drinking, leaving home, the housework, starting work. Be aware of the physical. As the day progresses, if you begin to feel under pressure *switch off* by following the breath, emptying the mind, letting go, changing the thought. Home in on the breath, the Big I, the alone.

ACTIONS SEEN AS RITUAL

The choice of actions that can become ritual is a personal one. The following suggestions are offered as a starting point.

Waking thoughts
Bowing to the beginning of a new day
Washing/shaving
Early morning meditation or a few minutes of quiet
   listening
Exercise performed as a hymn to life
Deep breathing exercises
A once a week home clean up or sorting out of your
   papers
Hand washing clothes (the ones that won't go in the
   machine)

Ironing, folding
Watering the plants
Gardening
Walking to work
Feeding the birds or a pet
Preparing a meal
Laying the table
Gratitude for the meal
Sharing a meal
Washing up
Putting away
Resting
Bathing, showering
Inner silence
Bowing to the end of the day.

THE ART OF ADAPTING TO CHANGE

Being open to change is freedom. A pitfall to avoid particularly if living alone or getting older is either rigidly holding on to fixed viewpoints or becoming too set in our ways. Adaptability means being open to change, both of heart and routine. Being flexible so that any disruptions to our lifestyle do not cause irritation.

Someone is coming to stay. The usual routine may have to be altered to accommodate our guest. Perhaps it will be necessary to eat at a different time, cook different food, stay up later, miss a favourite programme, wash at a different time, leave the bath clean. Rather than be irked by the thought of change, welcome it.

Our visitor arrives. They fling all their belongings around an immaculate space, or the chaos we enjoy is suddenly transformed by our well-meaning guest putting everything away. Don't get annoyed. Guests invariably pick up on irritation. See the humour of the situation by realizing how attached you have become to one way of doing things. Perhaps a day or two of chaos or order will be quite liberating. Everything can be put back or thrown around after they have gone.

Live spontaneously and the heart will never grow old. This is not to be confused with living unwisely or impulsively. The weather forecast predicted rain on Saturday. In fact it is a gloriously sunny day. Forget the ritual, forget the things you haven't done or mean to do. Jump out of bed and on to your bike, head for the station and catch a train to the sea. That's freedom.

LETTING GO

No matter how difficult or pressurized the day, get into the habit of giving yourself time to do something or appreciate something unconnected with work or problems, something that expresses your inner essence, something that gives you pleasure and expands a sense of being. Learn to let go and switch off from the problems of the day by being kind and firm with your over-taxed or anxious mind. Here are some ideas:

Meditation
Reading
Listening to music
Studying
Teaching yourself a language or to play an instrument
Writing a story or poem, keeping a diary
Painting, model making
Exercising at home
Walking to work/home
Cycling to work/home
Cooking
Gardening
Sport
Eating sandwiches in the sun
Star gazing
Resting, thinking about nothing.

FOLLOWING YOUR BLISS

As well as ritual we need to follow our bliss, celebrate, have fun. Following your bliss means doing all those things you want to have a go at but never got round to and following those wilder dreams which will require upheaval, a change of direction, a change of lifestyle. The motto for following your bliss is 'Go For It'.

This kind of behaviour has little to do with the gratification of material desires – sumptuous food, beautiful clothes, house, first-class travel, parties. Rather, it is following the inclination of the heart, using life creatively – which does not necessarily mean artistically. Artistically gifted people by no means have the monopoly on creativity. Perhaps letting go of all discriminatory thought is the most creative act any of us can ever do. In silence there is creation.

Following your bliss is freeing the spirit, not limiting or undervaluing yourself: 'I'd like to but . . .' 'I'm not clever enough to . . .' 'I'm too disorganized . . . too shy . . . too old . . . useless with my hands . . . no good at sport . . .' If you have a real yearning to do something, have a go.

Do the present physical, economic or environmental circumstances prevent you from pursuing a wilder dream? If so start with a smaller dream. The one that is within reach. Starting small may mean later the wilder one will also become a reality.

Life is short so the sooner we follow our bliss the better. Limiting and underestimating ourselves is in the past. Don't procrastinate; find a way to follow a smaller dream. If you want to rock climb, skate, ski, learn clowning skills, deep sea dive, fly a plane, parachute, ride a horse – find a way, have a go.

Maybe you want to visit Disneyland without children; at the age of forty skateboard down the high street; build a boat in your backyard; aged seventy register with a dating agency; at sixteen join a club for singles; or set up a group. Don't hesitate. Have a go.

Your wish is to start a collection, play an instrument, study Chinese calligraphy, cosmology, radically change your philosophy – do it. Start now. Following a dream is the point, not success or failure.

If you want to follow a dream that will mean radical change of direction, career, lifestyle or environment, you will need long and wise reflection, courage, vision – the ability to see beyond the immediate, trust in the inclination of the heart, being prepared for no safety net other than your own resourcefulness and independent nature (guaranteed security is an illusion anyway), exuberance, and trust that all will be well because you are now moving to the right track. If all these qualities are in place, be they somewhat wobbly, give a shout for joyous change and 'go for it'. What is right for you will ultimately be right for others.

Roam the world; live in another country; change your direction; your lifestyle; give up security for a more fulfilling dream; become a monk, a nun; live in a community; start up a business; be a hermit; change your job. Fly!

CELEBRATION

In Britain there are few opportunities for creative community celebration. The two main Christian festivals, Easter, and more particularly Christmas, have lost their honour to the pressures and distortion of consumer celebration. No matter how affluent, consumer celebration in any society invariably leaves in us a vacuum, a feeling there is something missing. Perhaps this is the reason why we are not always too good at knowing how to enjoy ourselves collectively. Yet many of us when we are invited to enjoy or take part in the street carnivals or festivals of other ethnic populations living here become like children. We join in with almost over-excited enthusiasm or enjoy the sights from the sidelines as smiling if somewhat wistful onlookers. Why? Because the spontaneous child inside the outwardly reserved Northerner has the opportunity to celebrate just for the sheer fun of it.

Creative celebration is about joy, gratitude, imagination, loving preparation, being able to make do with what is available.

Homemade Celebration

Celebrate to show that a day is important. Celebrating life costs nothing. Whether we live alone or with other people we can celebrate. Despite your own difficulties or deprivation you are someone generous enough to celebrate life. Creative celebration means reconnecting with the child's sense of wonder at the miracle of life. Here are some everyday things to celebrate.

Being alive and conscious
The greater
Being part of the universe
Being part of the human family
Good health
Nature
The seasons
Having kicked a negative habit or lifestyle
Having taken the plunge and got on to the right track
Your success or someone else's
Your good news or someone else's
A special event
Your birthday or someone else's
A New Year
A new day
A new job
A new friend
Connecting up with an old friend
You having transformed loneliness into the serene state
  of 'the alone'.

Here are some ways to celebrate alone.

Bow
Sing
Dance, exercise
Draw a picture, write a poem
Buy some flowers
Plant some seeds
Change a routine
Have a drink
Make a special meal
Dress in bright colours
Take yourself out for the day
Have a picnic
Stay in bed longer

Get up earlier
Smile all day

Daniel Dennet, an American arts and science professor writes in his book *Consciousness Explained*

Fun is not a trivial concept, but it has not yet, to my knowledge, received careful attention from a philosopher. We certainly won't have a complete explanation of consciousness until we have accounted for permitting us (and only us?) to have fun.

CHAPTER SEVEN

Coping with Acute Loneliness

It is not possible to understand the extent of another person's suffering because for each of us thresholds of pain differ. The pain of loneliness cannot be denied. Perhaps no book, however well intentioned, will provide definitive solutions for those overwhelmingly lonely moments. Yet our courage and ability to transcend profound suffering is quite remarkable. This chapter is offered in the hope that it will bring relief to anyone who may be experiencing a state of acute loneliness.

'My disability makes me entirely dependent on the good will of other people. When they don't come I feel terrible.' 'Sounds stupid but when my best friend at school didn't want to be friends I felt like killing myself.' 'I miss her so much; we shared forty years; nothing can stop that loneliness.' 'An eating disorder is a hidden illness, like a frightful secret. I sit on the bus looking at the people wishing I was like them. It is such a lonely feeling.' 'I have six months if I'm lucky. Friends are grand but you're on your own. On bad days it's like preparing to be swallowed up in a black hole.' 'I have no special problem. In fact I am really lucky. It's just that I'm desperately lonely.' 'Being rejected by someone you love is an unbearably lonely feeling.'

Never feel that loneliness is something you have to work through on your own. Never feel hesitant about asking for the support of other people. Asking for help is an act of generosity on your part because it allows someone else the chance to offer a hand in friendship or share their expertise.

If your courage is beginning to fail because so far the attempts to find friendship or support have been to no avail please don't give up. Keep a positive outlook even if at present it is somewhat of a strain. Tell yourself that the support you need will present itself in a way that is exactly right for you.

Feelings of loneliness are sometimes difficult to recognize yet they may be the cause of mental turmoil which manifests itself in the guise of an addiction or compulsive patterns of behaviour. The urge to drink, take drugs, gamble, steal, lie, fantasize, overeat, starve, become trapped in negative relationships, can all result from profound inner loneliness. Often this is the result of past trauma, in which case it may be very helpful to look at past feelings rather than immediate problems.

Each painful experience presents us with an opportunity to develop into a stronger person. With a brave heart let go of past pain – you don't need it any more. Resentment, guilt or blame are unproductive. Forgiveness is healing. Now you are your own person. If loneliness was and is a cause of your present distress, work from that premise. Allow other people the opportunity of working through the problem with you. With your head held high shout it from the rooftops: 'Yes I was lonely as a child, I didn't like to see what my mum and dad were doing to each other', 'My mum took more notice of her boyfriend than me and he had only just come', 'I was spoiled rotten but they were never there'.

Investigate the different kinds of support available – psychotherapy, counselling, self-help groups, doctors, spiritual friends. National directories on such subjects as counselling, psychotherapy and voluntary agencies (*see* Further Reading) provide useful data. Libraries and Citizens' Advice Bureaux house local directories with information on self-help groups, social support organizations and telephone helplines. Chapter 12 is devoted to practical suggestions and information that could bring contact with new people.

Information directly related to the condition of loneliness is not always easy to come by. Loneliness is not often spoken about but the sooner we are able to admit to loneliness without fear of being misunderstood the sooner the problem will be recognized as one needing direct attention rather than indirect attention. Many well-meaning organizations shy away from using the word lonely. There seems to be a stigma attached to the very word. Time and again it has been demonstrated that until the lid is taken off any distressing condition the sufferers not only undergo the pain of the condition but also, through fear of rejection, the pain of not being able to speak about it. Anyone who is lonely can help to bring about change by not being intimidated. Use the word lonely with your head held high. Maybe the day will come when we are positively encouraged to admit we are lonely and then people will begin to help each other and do something about it.

Many organizations, services and groups are indirectly concerned with loneliness. Some offer support for situations of extreme deprivation or illness; others offer friendship and human contact. Radio stations provide a wide variety of support programmes aimed at lonely people. Yet the framework for encouraging people to work their way out of loneliness is very fragmented.

Loneliness can make a person retreat into themselves with confusion and lack of confidence. To the outsider this may appear to be inertia. Often when a person is aware that they are lonely, they are unclear about what they need or are looking for to remedy the situation. For this reason there may be hesitancy to approach an organization with a vague query relating to loneliness. The individual may prefer in the first instance to have a resource that will enable them to look at the problem from their own surroundings and perspective until they have a clearer idea of a direction to take. As already mentioned, relevant national or local directories are good starting points. The support is there; it is a question of finding the kind you feel comfortable with.

WEEKENDS AND PUBLIC HOLIDAYS

'I can just about cope, but when it comes to weekends and public holidays I dread it. Everyone else seems to have someone or be going somewhere.' 'I try and make plans but the few people I know often cancel at the last moment. I suppose it doesn't matter to them but it does to me.' 'Now I'm unemployed weekends are the loneliest times; they just don't seem like weekends any more, just another day of the week.' 'Being homeless, weekends are the worst. Weekdays are not so bad – all the centres are open. Yes, the weekends are the worst.' 'I dread weekends. The "family-ness" of the whole thing makes me feel claustrophobic and very lonely inside. I know I shouldn't and that makes me feel guilty which makes it even worse.'

Weekends and public holidays are indeed difficult times if lonely and alone. The support agencies close down, everyone who could be a lifeline takes off. Everyone seems to be together or going off to do something exciting. Everyone except you seems to be looking forward to the holiday. Many people dread the prospect of a lonely weekend or public holiday.

Rather than force yourself to join up with people with whom you have little in common, it may be easier in the first instance to be by yourself, stay put and view the weekend or holiday as a time for catching up on all the things you never get round to doing.

Another strategy could be to plan the weekend or holiday in advance and make it a special time for you. 'Right, it's the bank holiday and I'm going to celebrate it in my own way. OK it may be lonely at times but it's better than forcing myself to be with people I don't really want to be with.' Rather than being hard on yourself, treat yourself by doing something, having something or going somewhere different. Get up later, earlier, prepare a special meal for the evening. If you live in a city, walk to a local café and read the papers. If you can afford it, take off for the afternoon, go to a sporting event, visit a garden, exhibition, go on a cycle ride, go to the cinema. Many people go to afternoon films alone. The great secret is to live in the present. The second day of the weekend could be a challenge to live in the moment and an opportunity to have an uncomplicated creatively tranquil day.

'Try being desperately lonely and doing all that. It's only too easy to say, but when I'm down all I want to do is crawl into bed.' On days when you feel very unhappy, ring someone up if possible and ask for their support. If there is no one, sustain yourself with great love. Send out goodwill to all the other people who might be experiencing loneliness at the same time. Remind yourself that the day will pass and that tomorrow is a new beginning, as indeed is the next moment.

Everything changes all the time even though you don't always notice it. Hold yourself dear, for you are dear.

Celebratory times like Christmas or New Year can be difficult for many reasons, but never more so than if you long to join a party and have no invitation to do so. For anyone who would like to be with other people but away from social pressures, the answer might be a retreat centre or spiritual community. You will not necessarily be expected to share the same philosophy or beliefs and many people go on their own. You will be welcomed, your privacy respected, and more than likely the surroundings will be healthy as well as beautiful – minimal costs and maximum kindness, and well worth exploring. Details will be found in *The Good Retreat Guide* (*see* Further Reading).

Voluntary work over Christmas can be fun as well as a rewarding thing to do. Not only does it help to ease someone else's situation, but it brings contact with other volunteers. Contact a volunteer bureau or a project such as Crisis at Christmas, well in advance of the holiday. If you have the funds, another idea to consider is an adventure holiday, such as trekking in India, or an archaeological or ecological expedition. Many of them span the Christmas break.

If none of these suggestions appeals or is possible, then gently close your front door on the world until the festivities are over.

HELPING YOURSELF AND OTHERS

Consider joining a weekly activity oriented towards health and well-being – a meditation or self-help group, yoga or relaxation classes. Join to meet new people whose common quest for peace of mind may perhaps open new doors for you.

The brightness of heart, the flower of the heart, is our birthright. Only we can protect that brightness from being dimmed. Never allow the flower of your heart to be crushed by difficulties, rejection or the negative words or actions of other people. Our own peace of mind will help other hearts as well.

Through our ability to be positive, to smile, to let go of past pain, to respect ourselves, to accept help gracefully when we need it, to work with what is and flow with change, we can help to heal ourselves, for these qualities ease the mind and soften the body.

Everyday qualities that help to heal other people are good will, an ability to cheer someone up, to reassure, to encourage, to share joys and sorrows, to rejoice in another person's good fortune. Other qualities that help to heal? Being able to forgive, to smile, to hug with love, to give full attention to whomever we are with, to avoid or turn a negative conversation or petty gossip into a positive direction.

Most of us are conditioned to the idea that real healing can only come from the outside through the expertise and remedies of professionals. So often we turn to the doctor, therapist, counsellor or social worker and, when all else fails, the spiritual healer. Are we aware of our own healing powers? More than likely any thoughts on this subject may have been dismissed as presumptuous or fanciful. A lay healer is often seen as someone special with supernatural powers yet in truth they are everyday people like ourselves, the only difference being they have discovered their green fingers and up until now we have not. You are special and so am I. You are part of the whole and so am I. You have the opportunity to discover your own green fingers and so do I. When we do we can help to heal ourselves and those around us.

'Do-it-yourself' healing needs to be approached with a light touch rather than serious determination to achieve a result. We are not talking about miraculous cures, rather about easing the mind, softening the body and instilling a sense of well-being. What works for one person may not for another.

The following exercises are offered as a springboard. They are all based on a similar theme, that of total attention and silent observation of the mind. Though the exercises are best practised sitting down in a quiet place, try them out wherever and whenever they are needed. The aim is to carry within us a still place wherever we are.

Exercise: Staying with the pain

In the first instance, should an overwhelming sense of loneliness or distress arise, close the eyes and stay with the pain. How does it feel right at that very moment, how does the body feel? Go right into the sensation and face it head on. How is it? Terrible? Stay with the terrible, don't analyse or judge – just be with that feeling. Rather than fight, deny or try to escape the pain, simply observe it from a position of grace and dignity, with the mind of the Big I.

Inhale deeply and exhale slowly. Stay in the now, not forwards or backwards. Breathe in and out, in and out. Terrible, terrible, less 'panicky', terrible, I'm not going to do this any longer – it doesn't work, terrible, terrible, peacefully terrible, it is beginning to dissolve into a quieter state . . .

The more frequently this exercise is put into practice the more power it has to relieve mental pain. In certain instances it will also relieve physical pain.

All kinds of secondary emotions can result from loneliness – jealousy, ill will, bitterness, compulsions towards food, drink or cigarettes – all of them cravings for comfort and the love, warmth and understanding we are not receiving or are not open to. The following exercise may help.

Exercise: Coping with negative emotions or compulsions

Sit still and observe these passing waves of thought energy – for that is all they are. Do not try to suppress them. Observe yourself with great tenderness, rather than dislike. You are watching the insecure frightened child within us all. Silently label the emotion 'envy', 'bitterness' or 'compulsion', then leave it at that. Stare these emotions in the face until they dissolve and you are left looking into an empty and peaceful space.

Negative patterns of thinking often reappear in different guises, rather like an itch wanting to be scratched. They seem to refuse to go away. The secret is to sit tight, stay with the moment and watch. From a position of neutrality, grace and dignity you let the thoughts and emotions go their way.

A different strategy for coping with negative states of mind is humour, as in the following exercise.

Exercise: Using humour

Acknowledge what is going on out loud: 'Today I am in a bad, mopey, negative mood. This is going from bad to worse. I started picking on Jane and I have ended up having a go at Lesley. How did he get into the story?' Or maybe it goes something like this: 'This is really over the top. I don't have a positive thought about anyone or anything, and I don't seem to be able to do anything about it. Why am I punishing myself like this? Never mind, tomorrow is a new day. Today? Well I'll just carry on being negative.' Often when the mind has given itself permission to think negatively, thoughts cool down because there is no one to fight with.

An alternative tactic would be to do as Louise Hay suggests in *You Can Heal Your Life*: 'Change the thought and the feeling must change . . .'

The following exercise is to test whether your habitual thought patterns tend to be mainly positive or negative. Try it out when you go for a long walk.

Exercise: Thought patterns

As the passing thoughts arise, notice whether they come into the negative or positive bracket. Label them 'positive' or 'negative' and leave it at that. Carry on walking, focus on your posture and your feet as they connect with the ground. When new thoughts arise, repeat the process. Whatever the results, don't criticize yourself. (Krishnamurti spoke of freedom through watching the mind with 'choiceless awareness'.) Once we are aware of habitual thought patterns, they can be changed. Whenever the exercise becomes a strain, stop and just enjoy the walk.

A chattering anxious mind is tiring but any attempt to still that activity may meet with protest from the mind, new thoughts diverting our attention by every means available. Try the following.

Exercise: Emptying an anxious mind

Experiment on another walk or whenever the mind is troubled or anxious. This time when any thoughts arise, both the good ones and the not so good ones, silently say the words 'let it go' and do just that. The phrase 'let it go' helps to neutralize the thought and distances you from it. Realizing we are in control brings a sense of freedom. As soon as the exercise becomes a strain, stop.

Exercise: Stilling the mind

Following the breath is a beautiful and effective way to calm the mind. Just sit and be aware of the body breathing in and out, in and out. Watch the breath enter the body and leave the body. When your mind calms, carry on living in the moment. From time to time turn your attention to the body. How does it feel at that very moment? Listen to the body; its advice is always related to the immediate.

FEAR

Thresholds of pain differ, thresholds of fear differ. Fear can be a terrible experience. It is a debilitating emotion. If we allow ourselves to be dominated by fear – frightened of people, frightened of change, of the unknown – we are vulnerable, open to abuse and exploitation. By confronting fear with courage it can often be overcome. Recommended is Susan Jeffers' book, *Feel the Fear and Do It Anyway* (see Further Reading). Becoming acquainted with fear before it arises may help you to cope with it when it happens. Practice this exercise for a few minutes on good days when all is well, and the following one at bad times.

Exercise: Familiarizing yourself with fear

Sit in a peaceful position and close your eyes. Let the body settle. Be aware of the body breathing. Say the word fear to yourself and focus on the word. See if any particular part of the body reacts to it. Stay with the word and go beyond it. Then repeat it again. Do only that – no analysis, no thinking. Just familiarize yourself with a word that describes an 'unpleasant feeling caused by danger or expectation of pain'.

Exercise: Coping with moments of fear

If sensations of terror sweep through the mind and body, confront them. Say to yourself, 'This is fear'. Focus on the heart
area, on the dip just below the base of the centre bone on the
chest called the sternum. Breathe in deeply, breathe out
slowly. Stay with the fear, go right into it. Hold on to the
breath for support; breathing in and out, in and out. Know
that the heart area can by-pass these sensations of terror.
Watch the fear and hang on. Your courage and brightness
of heart is taking you beyond what is upsetting the body and
mind. Everything may be trembling but you are travelling
beyond it. Watch yourself transcend fear.

VISUALIZATION

Use the following visualizations whenever you need to look
up rather than down, or when things get difficult. They can
be practised anywhere at any time. They can also help to overcome fear.

Exercise: Visualizing the 'flower of the heart'

Sit in a relaxed and upright position and close the eyes. For
a few seconds gently follow the rhythm of the breath and
allow the body to settle. Visualize a white flower resting in the
dip just below the base of the sternum, the area of the 'sacred
heart'. Imagine the back widening, the spine lengthening and
the chest opening so that the flower has room to open out.
Feel the purity of the flower, the innocence of the heart, the
place where the ageless child rests. Focus on the flower of the
heart, the whiteness, the brightness. Allow the body to
breathe gently. When other people are unwell or troubled you
can place them there with the flower of your heart.

Exercise: Visualizing a clear light

Sitting in an upright position with the eyes gently closed, for
a few moments be aware of the breath. Now visualize the
whole body being filled with clear translucent white light.
Visualize the bones, the whole of the skeletal frame, filled
with this light. The same light fills the skull and face. Visualize
translucent light in the skull. Sit there, basking in clear light,
with streams of clear light flowing through the body.

Exercise: Visualizing a crystal light

Sit in an upright position. Close the eyes. Breathe in peace, breathe out peace. Visualize a healing crystal light penetrating any part of the body that may hurt. Visualize the affected spot. It is now crystal clear. As you inhale, light is drawn down into the body; as you exhale, the purity of light heals. See yourself with a crystal body. Rather than focusing on the ill, see only the purity of light in yourself. Don't think 'will this or won't this work?' At this moment you are seeing your true nature – clear pure light. This exercise is based on a guided meditation in an Amaravati Buddhist publication called 'Seeing the Way' (*see* Further Reading and Useful Addresses).

Exercise: A guided meditation to bring sleep

Sit in an upright position. Notice if there is any tension in the face. Let the face soften. Let go. Let the attention rest in the heart area. Allow the breath gently to find its own peaceful rhythm.

Now when you breathe in say to yourself 'May I be well'. As you breathe out, hold the thought, 'May others be well'. Feel the heart opening as you wish yourself well; feel it opening as you wish others well.

Bring to mind those close to you. As you breathe in and out wish them well. Say their names. Say, 'May you be well.' Open your heart to them.

Visualize your parents whether they are living or dead. Wish them well: 'May you be well.' Breathe in and out, wishing them well. Then as you inhale and exhale return to wish yourself well: 'May I be well.'

As you breathe in, wish all those around you well: friends, teachers, colleagues, neighbours. 'May you be well. May you go well.' Return to wish yourself well: 'May I be well.'

Wish all those who may have harmed you well. Breathe in life and with an open generous heart wish them well: 'May you be well. May you go well.' Return to wish yourself well: 'May I be well.'

As you gently breathe in and out wish all beings well wherever they may be: 'May all beings be well wherever they may be. May all animals, insects, birds and plant life be well. May the universe be well. May all life go well.'

Breathing in and out, in and out, return to the heart: 'May I be well. May I go well.'

CHAPTER EIGHT

Reconnecting with the Body

This chapter explores how reconnecting with the body can alleviate mental stress.

For a short time each of us is an expression of the ever-changing universal life dance. For this dance we do not have to look a certain way, be a special shape or a particular age. We do not have to train to become dancers. Like it or not, we already are. Although surrounded by other dancers, each of us dances alone. When it all began and when it will cease is not for us to know. Tai Chi, an ancient Chinese form of movement, expresses this beautifully in the name given to a particular movement sequence – 'Cloud arms, no beginning, no end'.

In the West most of us need to learn how to live less in our heads and more with our bodies. Conscious thought is at least ninety per cent focused on 'me' and 'having to do'. The mind separates itself from the body and thought patterns become negative, anxious and confused. The energy circulating the body is then blocked which causes further stress and tension. Yet the miracle is the body breathes, repairs itself and slows down with age, all without conscious instruction from 'me'.

The pressures and demands of daily life can build up and cause us to feel as if all the energy is up in the head rather than freely coursing through the body. These are the times when it helps to turn our attention to the body and allow it to untie some of the knots.

The first step is not to underestimate ourselves. Bodies are miraculous instruments, microcosms of the universe. The body responds to love and reacts to aversion (I can't bear looking at myself . . . I'm too fat . . . too thin . . . too small . . . too tall . . . ageing and sagging . . . I'm not going to bother until I'm fatter . . . thinner . . .'). Berating ourselves is to deny our magnificence and hand over our power to the dictates of fashion.

Consider the body at a profounder level, as the instrument through which life flows, the loyal friend who puts up with an amazing amount of abuse ranging from diet to over taxing, that gallantly carries on even when the mind is in turmoil.

Reconnecting with the body means giving attention to posture, breathing patterns, inner rhythms, daily movements, balancing energy and the language of the body. If the following suggestions are reflected upon and put into practice, immediate benefits will be felt.

INTRODUCTION TO POSTURE

The basis for reconnecting with the body is finding the right standing and sitting positions. Once we have established the right posture for ourselves, we will be able to express our true nature more freely. The standing or sitting position will become an anchor to return to, a physical position where we can recollect ourselves, allowing the breath and energy to circulate and flow freely.

Many books have been written about systems devised for achieving a good posture. The Alexander Technique is particularly recommended (see Useful Addresses). The posture suggestions here are not definitive. They mainly consist of suggestions and visualizations which help you to find your own right standing and sitting position, according to the proportions of your body.

Little physical effort is required for posture. There is no need to 'yank' the body into positions, 'shoulders back', 'head up'. Our right posture has been with us all the time. All we have to do is reconnect with it. Therefore, try to adjust the body as little as possible. Instead, let the mind send messages or visualizations. If you keep practising, very soon the body will respond. The right posture will help the body to open and lengthen.

Standing

Stand with feet parallel, about a fist's width apart. Close your eyes and visualize your skeletal frame. Visualizing the skeletal frame can be a friendly experience. There is something endearing about a skeleton. (Should you be having a difficult day, perhaps being pushed about by a mass of people as you walk down the high street or being nearly run over by aggressive drivers cutting the traffic lights, try visualizing other people and yourself in skeletal form – nothing seems quite as serious as before.) Focus on three parts of the body: the feet, the lower abdomen and the crown of the head.

Open your eyes. Feel the feet going into the ground like roots. The weight of the body is between the legs and over the insteps. Feel that the heels and outside rim of the feet also take the weight of the body. Feel as if the little and big toes extend beyond themselves.

Travel up the legs to the knees; the legs should be straight without locking the knees. Feel as if the knee caps are also going forwards and away, extending beyond themselves.

Travel up to the hips. (Send a silent message to widen the hips and 'lift' the trunk off the hips.) Now turn your attention to your lower abdomen, often referred to in yoga as the 'hara'. This area is a few inches below the belly button. It is a storehouse of energy. Put some strength here by pressing the diaphragm towards it.

Travel up to the chest and focus on the sternum, the bone between the breasts. Allow the sternum to open as if uncovering a wide smile. Soften the chest. Just below this point you will find a little dip in the bone, which is sometimes referred to as the 'sacred heart'. It is a point where many emotions make themselves felt. Visualize the area of the sacred heart lifting up, radiating beams of light diagonally upwards. Our tendency when anxious is to close inwards towards the sternum. It is an involuntary protective movement, but in actual fact it only makes matters worse, as it blocks the natural flow of the breath.

Send a silent message for the shoulders to widen and visualize the weight of the shoulders resting on the arms and hips. Let the arms hang down by your sides so that the energy flows down to the tips of the fingers.

Travel up to the head. As a general guide the ears should be in a vertical line with the shoulders. Push up towards the sky with the back of the head. You will feel a lengthening at the back of the neck if you do this. Your chin will automatically tuck in. Many of us tend to pull the head back and jut the chin out, particularly when nervous or trying to prove a point. When the chin is pointing up there is no strength in the posture. Visualize the crown of the head supporting the sky. Your gaze should rest ahead of you at eye level. The level of gaze may feel strange at first if the habit has been to tilt the chin upwards.

Soften the facial muscles, soften the face. Let the corners of the mouth turn upwards in an imperceptible smile. Try often to cultivate this tiny smile, so that it becomes part of your expression. Smiling is now regarded even in the medical world as a movement that benefits the health of the whole body.

Now turn your attention to the heels and the back of the legs. Travel up the back of the legs to the base of the spine. Send an instruction to lengthen the spine. Visualize each vertebra having more room to breathe as the spine lengthens up to the temporal bone.

Visualize the spine as an expanding ladder helping the crown of the head to climb into the sky. Visualize the neck freeing the head so that it floats upwards.

Widen the upper back. Release and soften the rib cage so that it lets go of any tension. The rib cage is a part of the body which we often hold too stiffly.

Finally, return to the three points. Firstly, the feet and their relationship with the ground: silently say 'The power of the earth'. Then, the crown of the head pushing up into the sky: 'The power of the universe'. Lastly, the hara (lower abdomen) and its storehouse of energy: 'The power of humanity'. These three sentences may help you to keep in mind the three parts of the body to key into for a good posture.

Sitting

All the suggestions for the standing posture apply equally to the sitting position. For a correct sitting posture the body needs to be held upright (as described for standing). Allow the spine to lengthen. 'Slumping' is out. Our usual tendency when tired or depressed is to sink down. This only worsens matters. The vertebrae of the spine are crushed together, blocking the flow of breath. The mind and the body become even less connected. 'Slumping' can be a good feeling but from now on it has to be an occasional luxury.

Sit in an upright position, aware of the natural grace and dignity of the body. (That means you.) Shut your eyes and allow the face to soften. Visualize a translucent light filling the skull and the rest of the body. Allow all the parts of the body to soften and open out. Sit with the weight over the seat bones (the bony bit in each buttock). Put some strength into the sitting position by pressing the diaphragm down towards the hara (lower abdomen, two inches below belly button). Let any tension or exhaustion drain away through the face, the shoulders, the back, the arms, fingertips, legs and feet. Sit and be aware of the breath filling and emptying from the body.

Suggestions for Practice

Posture can be practised anywhere at any time, at the bus stop, in a checkout queue. Rather than anxiously wait, turn your attention to your posture. After a time the body will begin to adjust itself automatically. If you are depressed, focus your attention on the sternum (sacred heart area) and visualize it lifting upwards and outwards. Continue to focus on this part of the body. You may even find yourself smiling.

BREATHING

There are a number of different breathing techniques. Here the focus is on becoming more aware of our own breathing patterns so that the breath can be another anchor.

For the most part, the body breathes without instructions from the conscious mind. However, mental tension will almost certainly cause physical tension, which in turn interferes with the natural flow of breath. The breathing may become shallow and harsh or the breath is held. This is when it is necessary to step in and consciously breathe deeply, until the normal breathing pattern resumes by itself.

Shallow or harsh breathing is a result of breathing from the chest rather than inhaling through the nostrils and drawing the air down to the lower abdomen. If the breathing action is from the chest, the shoulders will rise up and down. This is incorrect. If breathing from the lower abdomen, the top half of the body remains still. This is correct. The following exercise is for deep breathing, which can be used as an anchor during mental stress or to relieve exhaustion.

Exercise: Deep breathing

Sit in an upright position on a chair or cross-legged on the floor. Fold the hands in the lap or rest them on the knees. Soften the face. Let any tension or tiredness drain out through the face, the back of the neck, the chest, the arms and hands, the legs and feet. Let the tension flow out from shoulders, the buttocks and the solar plexus (that vulnerable spot between the rib cage and abdomen). Listen and watch your breath. At this stage do not try to adjust it; just see what is happening. (Following the breath in a sitting position is the foundation of any meditation practice.)

Now turn your attention to the hara (lower abdomen). With the mouth gently closed, inhale through the nostrils and slowly draw the breath down to the lower abdomen. The stomach will inflate like a balloon. Exhale the air from the lower abdomen up through the body, so that it is expelled through the nostrils. The stomach will now deflate.

You could silently and slowly say 'filling' as you inhale and 'emptying' as you exhale. Another suggestion would be to inhale and exhale on the word 'now' or 'peace' or even 'now peace'. The exhalation should take longer than the inhalation. You will probably find there is a natural pause before inhaling again.

While breathing, concentrate on the breath or, if you find this difficult, on the movement of the abdomen acting as a bellows filling up and emptying out. There are many visualizations that can be used while focusing on the in and out breath. For example, filling the body with colour or light, or breathing in and out good will. At first, however, it is better simply to follow the breath, making sure the breathing action is coming from the abdomen.

When the shallow breathing has calmed down, say after six to ten deep breaths, allow the body to begin to breathe by itself again. Stay peacefully in an upright position.

WALKING

Being aware of the action of walking is a good way to reconnect with the body. Feel the strength in the legs as you walk. Notice how it feels as each foot connects with the ground. Notice the pace of the walk. Is it jerky or flowing? Are you digging the legs into the ground? Doing this places too much stress on the knees. Walk from the hip (rather like a cowboy) so that the knees go forward and away. Send a message 'lift off the hip, spine lengthen, neck free the head'. Let the strength of the upper body carry you along. Be aware of the space that you are moving through. Let go inside. Let go outside.

If you are walking in surroundings which cause an uneasy feeling, instead of being affected by the situation and getting caught up with the chattering mind – 'This is dreadful; why did I come?' – bring your attention to the feet, the walking movement, the lengthening of the spine, the strength in the back as the crown of the head pushes up towards the sky. Don't look down. Your gaze should rest gently ahead of you at eye level. The walk is now your personal dance.

Becoming more aware of our movements and their relationship with the earth and our surroundings is not really something new. It is more like reconnecting with forgotten friends.

BALANCE

A sense of balance is not merely being able to move into a complicated position or stand on one leg or your head for hours – wonderful experiences of course but only for people with a fine sense of equilibrium. Each of us has to work within the limitations of our body. It may be that co-ordination of movement and balance are not our strong points. Inner balance and outer balance go hand in hand. Being more aware of our inner rhythms, our breath, the way we walk, stand and sit creates equilibrium between mind and body. Most of the time we push our body into unnatural positions, for example when hurrying to catch a bus laden with shopping. The breathing has become shallow, and the body lopsided. Stop for a moment. If you miss the bus, you miss the bus. Say to yourself, 'inner balance'. Take a few deep breaths. Then continue.

ENERGY

According to the dictionary, energy is (1) The capacity for vigorous activity (2) The ability of matter or radiation to do work either because of its motion or its mass or its electric charge (3) Fuel and other resources. We, like everything else within the universe, are bundles of changing energy. Anxiety or unhappiness can cause the flow of energy through the body to be blocked; then there is either too little or too much, both of which are unpleasant feelings.

By becoming more aware of the body's energy as we move through the day, we can learn how to redirect and balance blocked energy. If you are in a state of exhaustion, shut your eyes and breathe in deeply, replenishing the body with energy. As you exhale let the exhaustion drain away with the breath. Repeat this a number of times, just focusing on the breath.

Energy can be redirected to help dispel a negative state. For example, anger can cause a surge of energy which knots itself somewhere in the body such as the solar plexus or abdomen. If this happens, sit down (if possible) and shut your eyes. Focus the attention on the physical feeling of the knot and stay with the sensation. Breathe in deeply. On the exhalation visualize that the knot of energy begins to soften and flow out.

We can enhance the well-being of others by radiating positive energy through the simplest of actions, such as a smile, the expression of the eyes, a gesture or greeting, and the way we carry ourselves, sit or walk. Radiating positive energy is healing not only for others but also for ourselves.

BODY RHYTHMS

Think about the pace at which you operate most of the day. Are you comfortable with this tempo or has it imposed itself because of outside pressures? Think of the different ways you walk or perform an action when you are anxious, afraid, depressed, happy, confident, calm. Notice the change of rhythm. From time to time 'step outside' yourself to take account of the way external pressures are affecting your natural inner rhythms.

Walk around the room at the pace you would choose to conduct your life if you had the choice. See if it is possible to keep to this rhythm for one whole day. Become more aware of the influence thought patterns have on the body's rhythm. Though we may have little control of the external conditions of our lives, we have the choice to pace ourselves as we wish.

BODY LANGUAGE

The language of the body often reflects the language of the mind. The body reflecting the anxiety of the mind does nothing to solve the problem, it only makes matters worse. If you discover the body reflecting a negative mental state, stop. Step outside yourself to see the physical picture. Connect with the three points: feet, head and hara (lower abdomen). Consciously adjust the posture so that the part of the body which was most reflecting the mind is no longer doing so.

Think of all the territorial movements our bodies make when we feel our space has been or is about to be invaded, such as when sitting in a railway carriage with a vacant seat next to us.

Once we are aware of our body language we can adjust it and speak through it. For example, you are being interviewed for a new job. You are nervous as you enter the room. Hang on to the feet and posture as an anchor. Feel the feet connecting with the ground, the spine lengthening. When you sit, very deliberately place yourself in a position that speaks of alert quietness, even if inside you are shivering. Take no notice if your would-be employer is slumped down or using the body like a corkscrew as he/she swivels around in the executive chair. Your body language is sending the message that you are your own person.

We make many unnecessary gestures through shyness, nervousness or uncertainty, for example when speaking on the phone and fidgeting or fiddling with this or that. Nervous movements can become unconscious habits which dissipate energy and attention.

DAILY PRACTICE

Routine activities such as cleaning the bath, making the bed or washing up demand different rhythms and movements. Full attention to the physicality of the task in hand quietens an anxious mind. Be aware of the muscles you use when making a bed, the action of the back when cleaning a bath, the stance of the body as you hoover, the strength of the legs and trunk as you reach up to put something away. How does the body feel as you walk upstairs? Every day each of us performs a new life dance.

RESTING

Give yourself time to rest and let go. Talk yourself (out loud) through some of the following relaxations. They can be done in bed, on a chair or on the floor.

Exercise: Four ways to relax

Lie on the floor. Let the floor support you. At this moment there is nothing you have to do. Just rest, let the body surrender to the floor. Let your feet 'undo' themselves and soften. Soften and rest the knees. Rest the thighs and the backs of the legs. Allow the buttocks to spread out and become part of the floor. 'Undo' the spine by letting each vertebra undo itself. Let go of the rib cage and let it soften. Soften the front and the back of the neck. Let the shoulders widen and flatten. Let the arms and hands 'undo' themselves. Visualize a translucent light in the skull. Let the brain empty and the mind rest. Soften the cheeks and mouth; let go of the jaw bones and the chin. Let go of the back of the neck and soften the throat. Follow the breath until you become one with the space around you.

Lie flat on the floor. Shut your eyes and breathe gently. Feel that you are lying on a soft fluffy pink cloud; rest your whole body in this cloud. Let each part of your body sink into the cloud. No part of your body needs to work – the cloud will support you. All your worries and tensions disappear through the cloud. Let yourself be empty. Lie there gently floating. Breathe gently, up and down, in and out, up and down, in and out. Relax your hands and your fingers, your feet and toes, the back of your neck, your chest, your buttocks, your stomach, the knees, the back of knees, the legs. Let everything else rest. Simply float. Listen to silence, become part of silence.

Lie on the floor with your eyes closed. Imagine you are lying on a beach. The sand is warm, the sun is shining down, the waves are lapping over the shore. Someone is very gently pouring warm sand over you. It trickles on to your face, your cheek, your neck. The warm sand runs down the back of your neck, your shoulders, the front of your arms, and you feel the back of your arms against the warm sand. The sand is pouring over your chest and stomach, down your back, your buttocks, down the front of your legs, your calves, your ankles, your feet, the soles of your feet. You are lying there absolutely relaxed with the sun warming you and your mind at rest.

Lie on your back, feet hip-width apart, arms at sides, palms, upwards, and breathe deeply. Close your eyes, breathe in for four counts, hold, and out for four counts. Focus on your breath and let all thoughts dissolve. None of the problems of the day concern you during this time of rest. Just let go. Release your toes, let go of your feet, your ankles, calves, knees, back of the knees, thighs. Let go of your buttocks and stomach. Relax and soften your chest, your diaphragm, your spine. Let go of the back of your neck, relax your eyes. Let your brain rest. Rest your heart, your stomach. Just rest. Lie and rest.

CHAPTER NINE

Reconnecting with your Surroundings

What we eventually discover in our passionate remembering of the galactic, terrestrial, biological and human stories is that a study of the universe is a study of the self.

Brian Swimme, cosmologist[1]

I think we are in more intimate, closer contact with nature when we understand more, not less. I think we become less self-centred, less obsessed, more mature and, above all, more imaginative when we understand our experiences. We become a conscious part of nature, neither above nor below it, with our own unique place in an interconnected universe.

Joe Schwartz, physicist[2]

Our present-day separation from so many natural processes can be an unconscious cause of profound inner loneliness. Feeling 'apart' and unrelated to our surroundings often results in a bewildering sense of isolation; we feel like a tiny piece of jigsaw that cannot find anywhere to fit. 'I do lots of things, but inside I feel so alone.' 'I hate doing nothing.' 'I always have the radio on for background noise.' 'Walking is boring unless there is something at the end of it.' 'The thought of retirement fills me with gloom. What will I do?' 'I go to lots of parties but sometimes I think "what's it all about?".'

How did this sense of apartness come about in the first place? Could one reason be those religious beliefs which put forward the idea that God created the world for the benefit of human beings? This taught many of us to think in terms of the right to take, superiority and apartness. Such thinking has often resulted in taking from nature without giving or putting back. We think we know best and when things do not work out the way we think they should, we feel frustration, anger and pain. Thankfully, now, our anxiety about the survival of the human race has caused us to begin to respect and bow to nature, rather than trying to work against it.

In the modern world technology gives us information about practically anything by remote control. We can watch the world on television and we can communicate by phone, fax or computer. Nevertheless local communities have become increasingly separated and many people's lives are now far more isolated. Gadgets and appliances designed to save us time do not necessarily reduce the stress of our lives or give us more time for each other: 'No time to pop round and see Gran; I'll give her a call instead.' Instant gratification, 'taking the waiting out of wanting' as one advertising slogan put it, cannot increase our enjoyment of the moment.

However, we should not be negative about humankind's miraculous ability to invent, probe, research, push further, break new records. Professor Stephen Hawking, who has transcended the limitations of a desperately debilitating wasting illness, is a legend in the field of astrophysics. He sees the day when science will 'know the mind of God'. Technology can provide more time for personal development and exploration. We in the Western world have more opportunities than ever before to use our lives creatively and imaginatively and to concern ourselves with the well-being of other people. If we ignore these opportunities the fault lies with ourselves and not with the inventor or the invented. It is a question of balance.

Whilst enjoying the fruits of technology we need to explore and understand our relationship with the rest of nature, so as to be in touch with all that surrounds us. Loneliness can be greatly relieved by re-establishing an affinity with our natural surroundings, both animate and inanimate – the sea, rivers, streams, puddles, mountains, rocks, stones, pebbles, shells, sand, soil, trees, plants, flowers, sun, moon, stars, air, elements. We do belong though sometimes it may not feel that way. We are not on earth by mistake. Each of us is here for a purpose. Understanding that we are not separate but related to all that surrounds us is the first step to renewing a relationship with nature. Thich Nhat Hanh in *The Heart of Understanding* says:

If you are a poet, you will see clearly that there is a cloud floating in this sheet of paper. Without a cloud, there will be no rain; without rain, the trees cannot grow; and without trees, we cannot make paper. If we look even more deeply, we can see the sunshine, the logger who cut the tree, the wheat that became his bread, and the logger's father and mother. Without all of these things, this sheet of paper cannot exist. In fact, we cannot point to one thing that is not here – time, space, the earth, the rain, the minerals in the soil, the sunshine, the cloud, the river, the heat, the mind. Everything co-exists with this sheet of paper. So we can say that the cloud and the paper 'inter-are'. We cannot just be by ourselves alone; we have to inter-be with every other thing.'

WAYS TO RECONNECT

Re-establishing our relationship with nature needs to be a gentle process. It cannot be self-consciously forced, approached as yet one more thing to do. To be able to enjoy, observe and listen, hear the underlying stillness of wherever we are, we need at least temporarily to put aside the clutter of the mind. Become clutter free – like the birds. City birds seem oblivious of city chaos, city sounds, screeching car brakes, wailing sirens. City birds just carry on singing. They don't even need to pack when the time comes to fly halfway across the world. Our minds can fly to even greater destinations. If we put aside our mental clutter we don't need to pack either.

Reconnecting means having the time to notice. To see the little streetwise weed flower that has pushed its way up through the cracks in the pavement, the soft moss on a decaying building. Having the time to enjoy watching life in the form of animals, insects and birds. Ten minutes each day devoted to observing, listening and enjoying nature can nourish the human heart. The sense of belonging may not be rekindled overnight, but with patience and commitment it will happen. When it does, life will never seem as lonely as before.

Things to Enjoy

Trees never pick or choose who sits under them. When walking past trees breathe in deeply because trees replenish. Breathe in soothing healing green. Breathe, don't think.

Enjoy flowers – brilliant red, gentle pink, joyful yellow, transparent white, orange that sings to deep purple. Let colour reach out to the eye, rather than the eye to colour. Join the colour. Smile, don't think.

What about sweet smells? Wallflower, lavender, lilac, roses, herbs or newly mown grass, a bonfire, the sea. Sweet smells can never be captured. They belong to the whole; so do we.

The ground is one of our 'relations', the one that holds us up. Ashes return to the earth. Only passing clouds conceal the clear bright blue sky. Only passing thoughts conceal the mind's sky. Look up at moon and stars – we too are out there. The silence of mountains speaks if we have time to hear. Stones never complain of their smooth or jagged histories.

Water is our closest relation – our bodies are seventy per cent water. Let streams do the chattering. Rivers go with the flow; so should we. They make it home to the sea; so can we.

Sands welcome all travellers. Listen to shells, collect them, then leave them where they belong. The wind blows change; when the wind happens to blow, happen with it. The gentle breeze touching the face asks to be heard. Rain brings life-giving wetness. The sun is our oldest ancestor, a dying star which left behind the earth. At this moment we are spinning around the sun at a rate of 18.5 miles per second. Eighteen miles in the blink of an eyelid yet we never wobble. The seasons – here again? The universe lives in the now, so must we.

Things to Do

Walking is freedom. Walk wherever possible where there are trees and greenery. From time to time for a split second stop to hear the underlying stillness – life in the earth, life in the grass, life in you. On a sunny day, lie on your back under a tree. Look up through the leaves at a clear blue sky. This could be what is meant by paradise. Sit with your back against a tree trunk. Lie on grass or sand. Let every anxiety float away. Take a day trip to the sea or the countryside.

Garden, plant something, grow herbs in a window box. Ring up the council and ask for an allotment. Jim says that when he gets on to the allotment he becomes 'his inner man'.

Take a boat on the river. Sit by a river. Fly a kite. Take a lunch hour in the park. Cycle in the countryside. Put the bike on a train and just go. Learn to rock climb, ski, mountaineer, swim.

Help on a farm. Take a fruit-picking holiday – pick grapes, strawberries, hops. Go on a camping, sailing, trekking, horse riding holiday.

Sweep up the autumn leaves.

The following observations by astronauts are taken from *The Home Planet* edited by Kevin Kelley.

During a space flight, the psyche of each astronaut is reshaped. Having seen the sun, the stars, our planet, you become more full of life, softer. You begin to look at all living things with greater trepidation and you begin to be more kind and patient with the people around you. At any rate that is what happened to me.

Boris Volynov, USSR

From space I saw Earth – indescribably beautiful with the scars of national boundaries gone.

Muhammad Ahmad Faris, Syria

The Earth was small, light blue and so touchingly alone, our home that must be defended like a holy relic . . .

Aleksei Leonov, USSR

I talk about the moon being a very holy place.

James Irwin, USA

CHAPTER TEN

Perspectives of Loneliness

LIVING ALONE

Living alone may not be the first choice, but rather the way things have worked out; if the sting is loneliness, the nettle can be firmly grasped by viewing the situation as an opportunity for personal growth. Living alone need not mean a lonely life, as many people who previously dreaded that prospect discover. To avoid living alone one woman had been involved in a series of destructive relationships. Finally she had to take the plunge and learn to live alone – 'Well actually there was no choice' – and says that now she would be loath to swap her present lifestyle for round the clock togetherness.

Encouraging articles appear in the national press written by journalists who find themselves single again. They focus on the positive aspects of living alone, the freedom to pace their lives as they wish. These positive views help to change attitudes towards the single person.

There are indeed advantages to living alone, but care needs to be taken not to paint too glossy a picture. It is so much easier to live alone if you happen to be a gregarious, popular, busy person with good health and a reasonable income. The heartache of loneliness for many vulnerable single people has to be recognized as well. Ill health, a disability, personality factors such as lack of confidence, shyness, or low self-esteem, unemployment, poor environment, lack of money, racial harassment, being housebound, caring for an ill dependant, are all situations which can make going it alone a daunting task.

Few of us are designed for a solitary life, certainly not whilst young. Life is lived in relationship to other people – family, friends, colleagues, acquaintances, the passer-by. Each of us is born with the spontaneity of the ageless child who longs to smile, share, support, enthuse, enjoy and learn. On the other hand, until each of us is able to be an island unto ourselves we cannot truly be our own person. For only then can we live from a position of grace and dignity, no longer harmed by the negative words and actions of other people or the whims of fortune. Living alone provides the perfect opportunity to learn to be self-reliant. When we are our own best friend we are best friends for other people.

Learning to be self-sufficient does not mean hiding away. On the contrary, it means re-emerging with an even brighter heart. Living alone and lonely? Are you in danger of sealing yourself into a solitary life because of the hurt of loneliness? Do you duck out of arrangements, cancelling at the last minute? Do you change your mind a hundred times as an opportunity passes by? If these patterns sound familiar, they have to stop. Please do not shut yourself away. What may have begun as self-protection often becomes a habit which is increasingly difficult to break. Withdrawing into a cocoon, particularly when young, is no good. The spontaneity of your life is blocked, and other people are prevented from enjoying the brightness of your heart. 'Well no one wants my heart anyway, that's the problem, that's what it's all about.' 'Not now, next week maybe, I'm no company at present.'

Social occasions are not the only way to share yourself with other people. There are many other routes to explore. Chapter 12 makes a number of suggestions. Once you have pointed yourself in the right direction, good things begin to happen. A ripple-on effect starts, one opening leading to another.

Make one more courageous effort. Resolve to step out and fully participate in the life around you. Resolve not to retreat when the going gets tough. Life is not easy for anyone. Perhaps it is not meant to be. It changes from moment to moment. Like the weather there are stormy times and blue sky times. If we cling to the blue sky times and allow storm clouds to knock us over, we hand over our power and are no longer our own person. Meet the challenges without wobbling or, if you wobble, bounce right back again. If happiness which relies on other people and external conditions were true happiness, it would remain fixed. It does not. Like unhappiness it comes and goes. Rather than regard the down times as a personal affront, your fault, your fate, see in every experience a teaching. Cultivate humour and the lasting happiness of an unshakeable heart.

MEN AND LONELINESS

This book is addressed to both men and women but because of a frequent misconception that loneliness is a more common problem for women than men, it is necessary briefly to consider how it affects men.

'Men are all right, they have the pub and sport. It's easy for them to make friends' (married woman living on a housing estate). 'Everyone wants to invite the single male, not so the single woman' (female and divorced).

Socially, men on their own usually have an easier passage than single women. However, this can leave men feeling they should not be lonely because they have no cause to be. Few men feel able to acknowledge their loneliness and speak about it. If, on the rare occasions they do, it is invariably seen as personal failure, their fault, their social inadequacy. In extreme cases these fears result in harmful patterns of behaviour. To prove you are one of the crowd, or to forget that you are not, drink, gambling, drugs and sex become addictive substitutes which destructively cover up a sense of profound inner loneliness.

Less dramatic but no less distressing is that common feeling of isolation and apartness. 'My kids don't talk to me the way they do to my wife. I feel excluded.' 'In the evening I settle down to be on my own and then I can't take it. I go down to the pub, then I wish I hadn't gone . . . Yes, I have friends but ever since I was a child I have had this feeling of apartness. Why, I don't know. I had what I consider were the perfect parents.' All these sentiments were expressed by men with busy and successful working lives. The following extract from *The Guardian*[3] takes the idea further:

Men in general have yet to succumb to the notion that a problem shared is a problem solved . . . In America GO is the only men's magazine with a problem page; readers write in with their own particular anxieties. 'For what formal occasion can a blazer be worn?' 'Can gold and silver be worn at the same time?' This is hardly on a par with the psycho-sexual soul baring found in the problem pages of the women's press. In a world of ever changing sexual identities and roles, men have lagged far behind women in terms of defining themselves and expressing their feelings.

Though there is still a long way to go, attitudes are beginning to change. Women can help to speed up this process, rather than continuing to fall for the media's conventional stereotype of a successful attractive going-places never lonely man. Women need to understand that men too can be lonely; to recognize, encourage and value men's nurturing qualities. The ageless child within has no gender. Gentleness, sensitivity and spontaneity can be fostered in everyone.

The attitude of the male professional needs to change as well. For example, how many male general practitioners allow their own nurturing qualities to be seen by a male patient? Loneliness is acknowledged by many doctors to be a huge social problem but when referring to it the cited examples are nearly always female. How many lonely men with average to good circumstances feel able to make use of the therapeutic or counselling support that is available? Not many, particularly if it is only to seek help for loneliness. Usually it is thought easier to wait until a more specific problem arises, one that can be easily understood. In certain instances there is justification for such hesitancy. Not all professionals are sympathetic to the subject of loneliness. There may be a tendency to write it off as a human condition and move on to a more tangible problem, one that in fact may have been caused by loneliness. Happily there are many more therapists or counsellors who are only too glad to work through this problem with anyone who seeks their help. As one female psychotherapist said, 'If we see a man waiting in the corridor we practically fight to have him as a client.'

Support groups for men are emerging. Robert Bly's *Iron John* and Vic Seidler's *Men, Sex and Relationships* (*see* Further Reading) are among a growing number of books encouraging men to let go of who they think they should be and get on with being who they really are. Nowadays children's books bend over backwards not to stereotype parental roles, though the bias often seems to be in favour of the liberated working Mum and Dad and gets to sound like a real bore.

The most successful and privileged of men may experience loneliness. Perhaps the more successful you are, the more difficult it becomes to acknowledge. Just because you wear a suit and carry a briefcase, broke a world record, scored more goals than anyone else, are seen as an academic giant or a brilliant politician, do not ignore the flower of your heart. For if you do, even though you may not be lonely now, some day you will be.

TEENAGE LONELINESS

This section is devoted to the comments of young people who joined in discussions on the subject of loneliness and how it might affect their lives or the lives of other young people. The first discussion took place at a mixed comprehensive school with students between the ages of fifteen and sixteen. Their backgrounds reflected the ethnic mix within Britain. The second discussion took place at a girls' comprehensive school with three seventeen to eighteen-year-old students. None of the students took part because they were lonely, but because they volunteered. No one was asked if they were lonely, it was assumed they were not. Their comments were always perceptive, sometimes hilarious, sometimes poignant.

Two particular aspects of loneliness were highlighted. One was the fear of not having a friend or friends. The idea of doing things on your own was greeted with horror. Second was the deep and unspoken feelings of loneliness which arose when parents split up and a new boy or girl friend came on to the scene, someone who in their view then seemed to take pride of place over them.

Fifteen to sixteen-year-olds

'Wouldn't want to go to a football match on my own, boring.'
(Boy)

'Must have friends to share things with, jokes you know . . .' (Boy)

'Yeah I wouldn't go travelling alone. I mean it's no fun, suppose you are on the train and you fart. There's no one to have a joke with is there?' (Boy)

'Sometimes young people are lonely because they're different, they wear different things – you know, suits and ties.' (Boy)

'Sometimes they get lonely because of their politics. – was an out and out Tory. He kept telling us he was. It got a bit much.' (Boy)

'I'd rather be with someone I didn't like than on my own.' (Girl)

'Lonely kids try too hard. Not their fault.' (Girl)

'You make new friends through friends.' (Girl)

'No, I wouldn't tell another person if I was lonely. I mean you can't can you?' (Boy)

'No, I never want to be on my own. I always want to be with other people, any rate until I'm a really old man.' (Boy)

'Yeah there's pressure to have a girlfriend. If you haven't, well you're not one of the crowd.' (Boy)

'Home situations can make you really lonely, particularly if your Mum has a new boyfriend and things like that.' (Boy)

'Parents are very important in our lives.' (Girl)

'Yeah my Mum comes home and she asks her boyfriend if he's had a nice day. Doesn't ask me – that hurts.' (Boy)

'Sometimes I just want to talk to them, not sit in my room. But there's my sister with her boyfriend and my Mum with hers. I get on with him but it's lonely.' (Boy)

'I get lonely when Mum comes home late. There's nothing to do, just sit and watch the telly.' (Girl)

'My Dad is always nice to his girlfriend even when it's her fault. That's because he doesn't want to be lonely again.' (Boy)

'My Dad would tell me I'm selfish if I told him a newcomer has all the attention. He always says "Did you have a good day?" to her before me.' (Same boy)

Question

'Would you mind if your Mum came in and asked your Dad if he had had a good day, before she asked you?'

Reply

(Group almost in unison) 'That's different.'

'I mean you know they both love you and will stay.' (This remark was interesting because it was made by one of the students from a broken home.)

'There aren't enough places to just meet. We can't go to pubs. Youth centres are full of little kids.' (Boy)

'Cities are more lonely than country places.' (Girl)

Question

'Would it help if you were encouraged at school to be more on your own so that you could learn to enjoy your own company?'

Reply

'How can you enjoy your own company? I mean it's boring.' (Boy)

Question

'Do you think loners, those who prefer to be on their own, are thought of as strange?'

Reply

'Yes, if you see someone walk around the playground on their own you think there must be something wrong with them. That's why they haven't got any friends.' (Boy)

'My Auntie is 67 and she's ill so she's gone to a home. Well we said we'd go and see her every week. No one ever has.' (Girl)

'My Gran's in a home, she's 87. She's lonely but we don't go and see her. I don't know why – we just don't.' (Girl)

Seventeen to eighteen-year-old girls

'Yes loneliness is a problem for young people. You can be lonely even if you have friends.'

'If I heard someone say they were lonely I'd feel pity which is rather condescending. But you also wonder *why* are they lonely?'

'Some kids, thirteen year olds, feel pressurized into taking dope and that kind of thing. Maybe they don't want to, but if they don't they aren't part of the group.'

'It's easy to make friends outside school if you do something. I play in an orchestra so that's the way I make friends.'
'I'm quite lonely. I'm just not very good at making friends. I don't know why.'

Question
'Should there be more encouragement in school to do things on your own?'
Reply
'Well, there is a danger here. If you are encouraged to do things on your own you may use that as an excuse not to bother to try and make friends. Has to be a balance.'

'Yes, my Mum is on her own and I think she's lonely. That makes me lonely in a way.'

Question
'Do you talk to anyone about this?'
Reply
'Yes, my teacher. It helps in a way but I think it's better to talk to someone you don't know.'

'My Gran is lonely. She doesn't tell me because she doesn't want to burden me. I visit her once a week; Dad goes three times. She doesn't want to live with us, she wants to cook for herself.'
'I wouldn't tell a doctor I was lonely, he'd think I was wasting his time. Hardly like to tell him what's wrong with me when I'm ill, he seems so busy.'
'Certainly wouldn't go to a dating agency or answer a *Time Out* advertisement. Single holidays seem a good idea. Yeah I might go to a single club, I might . . .'

What Adults Can Do to Help

When you are young the whole fun of life is to do things in a gang or with a mate, so the fear of being friendless and having to do things alone is understandable and healthy. The problem is that these fears often carry on into adulthood. The result can be a profound sense of loneliness and failure if the time comes when it is necessary to stand alone with little preparation to meet this challenge, or encouragement to understand the value of learning to be self-reliant.

Group pressure begins at an early age. The loner at school is often looked upon both by staff and pupils as strange, and at home parents worry. Of course we all wish to see our children as popular and enjoying life with other young people, but sometimes parents place too much emphasis on having friends. When the child or teenager temporarily finds themselves friendless they mind not only for themselves but because they feel they have let their parents down. They are not a social success. How many of us have the wisdom to support our child through the pain of not being 'best friends' or 'one of the gang' and help them to see the positive aspects of being alone? Usually frantic efforts are made to compensate. We suggest they ring up someone else, we organize an outing, anything rather than help our offspring learn to enjoy being alone. As parents we are showing our own fear of loneliness. We have taken their loneliness on board.

Parents and teachers need to encourage children from an early age to become self-reliant and to enjoy their own company. Doing this will help to prevent the distress of loneliness in later years. Older students could be invited in the classroom to discuss loneliness as both a social problem and in relation to their own future. They need the wisdom of older people to point out the advantages as well as the disadvantages of being alone. As future adults their own ideas on how to combat the problem are important. The media could also play its part. Television and film advertisements always portray the young and successful as party-going and surrounded by friends. Do they realize how untrue these images are for many young people? Maybe sometimes they could show someone having fun on their own?

Whether we are good or bad parents, few of us understand just how important we are in the lives of our children, particularly during their formative and teenage years. They may not act as if we were, but we are. We are their Mum or their Dad. The pain of a parent leaving the home is bad enough. The pain of feeling you have to compete with the new boyfriend or girlfriend for affection is too much. Maybe the child's perception of the situation is distorted, maybe not. Either way when a newcomer arrives on the scene it is crucial to reassure our children that they are and always will be very special. It is crucial at such a traumatic time not to let them feel left out but rather to feel particularly loved and important. Of course, it is not always easy. Children from broken homes can try every trick of the trade to exploit the situation, at least until they feel safe again. Adolescents can be impossible, even at the best of times.

Perhaps as a single parent you are afraid of loneliness and feel an overburdened new partner may move away unless they have your undivided attention. Perhaps your new partner senses this fear and intentionally or not exploits the situation. If there is a conflict of loyalties, it must rest with our children. We must never give up on them for we are their lifeline to happiness.

CHAPTER ELEVEN

Social Loneliness

ENVIRONMENT

It is said that people are reflections of their landscapes; are we not also reflections of climate? Northern people from cold and wet climates are usually more reserved than those who live under a bright sun. The quality of daylight influences both mood and behaviour. In the sunshine we open like flowers; on grey days we tend to be more serious. When it is cold the body contracts; in the heat it expands. Warmth and bright light may relieve loneliness; cold and greyness can accentuate the problem.

Loneliness is a phenomenon of the affluent West rather than the East. The condition hardly exists in less economically developed countries – places where there are no state safety nets, where whole families live on the pavement, where abject poverty is rife. Perhaps the extended family and the common bond – a preoccupation for survival – prevent loneliness. Or is it religious underpinning, unshakeable beliefs which make you accept your lot humbly, which knits people together? Is it that the sun shines nearly all year long, or is it a state of mind? Who knows? One thing is clear, despite untold hardship, a lot more smiling goes on on that side of the world.

This is not to suggest that all in the West is gloom and doom. Not at all; there are many positive wholesome aspects and developments in Western society not found in the East. The truth is, both East and West have a long way to go.

Have the environmental planners in Britain paid enough attention to the relationships between people in an organized community and taken into account our climate and changing social structures – the breakdown of the family unit, working women, more leisure time? Are they aware there is a national problem of loneliness? It is doubtful. Should the thought have crossed one or two minds, more than likely it was dismissed as having little to do with environment and all to do with the therapist.

Environmental conditions can accentuate or relieve loneliness. High-rise flats where the lifts don't work, and where people are afraid to go out at night, once-vibrant communities now paper-littered ghettos, large terraced houses converted into as many anonymous sardine-box flats as space will allow, cities where shop fronts become night shelter for blanketed forms, rural areas with little or no transport and few facilities for the young, green spaces eaten up by developers: these are all environmental conditions which can cause people to feel alienated and isolated. 'Nobody cares, so why should I?'

Planners must recognize the problem of loneliness, for they could help to encourage friendship and prevent isolation. It is not more money that is needed but more sensitivity.

Cities where 'dreamers' are welcomed make city life far more relaxed and friendly. 'Dreamers' can be young or old, rich or poor. In many European cities you can stop at a pavement café for a coffee or drink and read your paper or just watch the world go by. No one pounces on you, telling you there is a minimum charge. In China it is the tea house, where families and neighbours meet and stay as long as they wish without feeling their welcome is dependent on their purse. Fast-food cafés are no substitute, for here the message is eat or drink up and pay.

A city that does not go out of its way to welcome children is a lonely city. Many cities all over the world regard children as important, and they are seen and welcomed everywhere. In the evenings the family goes out as a family to drink or eat. They know they will be welcomed by both patron and customers. Society has reached a low ebb when it becomes indifferent about the quality of life and environment it provides for the very young. Is it then surprising that when those children become adolescents they too may have developed the same shell of indifference?

Could a supermarket become a meeting place for single people in Britain? It has happened in America. It began when gay people found themselves frequenting the same well-known chain store. Pushing their trolleys around with the genuine intent of purchasing groceries, they began to converse with other gay people. What better way to meet people than over the price of a can of soup? No one loses out or feels rejected. If it looks like the makings of friendship you take it from there, otherwise it remains an animated discussion about shopping and 'have a nice day'. Word spread around. Gradually the younger heterosexual population picked up on the idea. Could that happen here, or are we too reserved? Would the innocence of the idea be abused? Would the management disapprove?

AGE GROUPS

Eighteen to thirty-five

In spite of the fact that our society is becoming more mobile and less class conscious, remnants of the old closed attitudes and habits remain. Social structures which have not changed with the times do little to help us become a less inhibited, more outgoing people.

Do not let a somewhat friendless situation erode your self-confidence. It is not your failure, rather a failure of the society you live in not to have created a free-flowing and welcoming environment and social structures which make it easy for people to interact with each other. Never feel ashamed of being lonely. Particularly if the non-lonely person finds it hard to understand how anyone young and healthy and mobile could be lonely: 'I mean, there are plenty of ways to meet people'. In theory yes, but in practice it does not always work out that way.

We can be lonely for so many valid reasons. It is not easy to meet our 'other' family (*see* Chapter 3). Many younger people suffer the loneliness of wishing to meet new people and not knowing how to do so. The ambience of the pub or wine bar may not appeal, particularly if you happen to be a rather shy person. If the truth were told everyone would like to make new friends, yet it can be difficult to find even *one*. It can be a lonely feeling to find we no longer have much in common with our old friends. People change, outlooks change. Some of us are happy to remain with those friends we grew up with, others have to move on. But how? We have split up with a partner and mutual friends have dropped us or we them: 'Help – where and how can I build up a new social life?' Hopes are placed on the new job as a potential source for meeting people. As it turns out the department is small and everyone is over the age of forty-five. 'The singles holiday was great, full of nice people. The problem was that when it was over everyone went their own way which happened to be a hundred miles from where I live.'

If the social life that you need has not yet come into being, be positive and know that it will. There is nothing selfish or manipulative in exploring every avenue that may lead to that 'other' family. On the contrary it is your responsibility to do this. It means you acknowledge and respect your own needs. Realize your other family is out there looking for you. Yes, looking for you.

View a social life in its broadest sense rather than just the social round. Be open to each new experience whether it is good or not so good. To do this requires a mixture of patience, perseverance, positive thinking and the courage to take considered risks. Despite shyness or the knocks of disappointment, risk more until you have built up a fulfilling social life. Risk bowing to the 'greater' and asking out loud for help to do this. Even if you have no specific feeling or faith, risk bowing. Greater there is, for at this very moment we are travelling around the sun at eighteen miles per second and still not losing our balance.

The next chapter offers a number of practical suggestions, including the introduction agencies and the singles club.

The middle years

People in their middle years often become lonely because this is a time when our lifestyle begins to have to change. The family has grown up. We are entering a different phase yet we are not quite sure of the direction it will take us. People in their middle years often fall into the trap of living out other people's images of a middle-aged person. As a nation we have a hang-up about age which can be a cause of loneliness for both elderly people and those in their middle years.

Middle-class people often find it particularly difficult to admit to loneliness. They tend to feel they should not be so since their circumstances may be more privileged than many others. Loneliness has little to do with advantage or disadvantage, particularly if you happen to come up against a social brick wall.

Much of the social support available is aimed at disadvantaged groups of people, but this is balanced by the exciting and varied adult education programmes open to anyone. Adult education centres are invaluable for the prevention of loneliness. These places provide a welcoming environment for learning and the opportunity to meet people from all walks of life. Their recipe prevents students being pigeon-holed either by age or background. There is something very attractive about the idea of going back to school as an adult.

Never feel socially inadequate if you are lonely. You do not have to grit your teeth and stick it out for the rest of life; other people need you, your attractiveness, your wisdom, your kindness, your bounce. Share your skills and your heart. Explore, study, enjoy. Put out a hand of friendship. Pioneer to change people's attitude towards loneliness. Live in the present and follow your heart.

Sixty plus

Lack of respect towards older citizens is shameful in any society, and is a cause of loneliness for many elderly people. Older people are discriminated against in practically every walk of life. The healthy mobile older person who has much to offer a community is rarely invited to be useful. The frail elderly person is either ignored or seen as a problem and treated like an infant. The successful retired professional or business person is regarded with more respect, and often invited to share his/her wisdom by sitting on committees participating in enquiries and so forth. Not so the everyday elderly person who may also have a wealth of experience and knowledge. His/her potentiality to be useful is largely ignored.

The very young and the very elderly have no problem in relating to each other. The rest of the community often tends to be impatient, condescending or indifferent towards the elderly. Watch how we/you react, when an older person takes time to pack up their provisions or find the right change at the supermarket check-out counter. What could be more destructive than these attitudes? Few day centres or clubs for elderly people, provide an intellectual and creative atmosphere. As one woman said, 'If I were the Bingo type I would be all right.' Singalongs, paper hats or constant television even when no one is watching are an insult to many older people. Charitable and professional workers who assume this is what they like are totally out of touch. Yes, this is what some people like but all those who don't have silently retreated. The population of older people in Britain is greater and more motivated than ever before. Our sensitivity to the intellectual, social and creative needs of people whose input has contributed to today's society needs to increase dramatically.

If you are older remind yourself each day of how much you have to offer the family, a friend or the community. Your experience, deportment, wisdom and values are desperately needed. Do not let anyone tell you otherwise. Pioneer for change. Join up with other like-minded people and become an articulate political and social force. Stand up for the ill or frail elderly person. In the USA older people have discovered their power: they are a force to contend with. One group called themselves 'The Grey Panthers'. They lobbied to great effect for the rights and dignity of senior citizens.

If the public, the government, the social worker, general practitioner, or the charity working for elderly people continues to discriminate, patronize or treat you like a problem child, protest. If they fail to provide the right environment and conditions for the brightness of your heart, join with other people and protest. Write to the press, the television or your local radio station. Start your own monthly discussion group, perhaps each month in someone else's house. So many older people are lonely, someone has to get the ball rolling. Perhaps it will be you. If there is something you would like to do, but you think it seems unsuitable at your age, don't worry – go for it.

Should you be someone who in the autumn of their life finds it increasingly difficult to live 'in the world', gently close the door and be at peace with your own company. Enjoy this moment, and then the next one and the one after that.

PEOPLE WHO ARE HOUSEBOUND OR DISABLED

People who are housebound or institutionalized are often the most forgotten members of society. 'The only person I ever get to see is the health visitor. I really look forward to her visit.' 'My problem is, darling, I'm deemed unfriendly because I haven't met a kindred spirit in this home.' 'When I was driven here in the ambulance and I saw the name of the place written large as life "Home for The Incurables" I never felt so alone as in that moment.' That last comment points to an example of the outdated structures mentioned above. At the beginning of this century when many of these institutions were founded the name 'Home for The Incurables' would have seemed appropriate. It reflected the public's view of chronically ill or severely disabled people – helpless victims who but for the grace of charitable support would not be cared for; a mixture of patronage and sympathy.

No longer do chronically ill people, particularly the younger ones, see themselves as victims. They are intelligent motivated people who wish to lead interesting, stimulating and social lives. Younger people with Parkinson's disease, multiple sclerosis or paralyses due to accident manage to transcend their bodily disrepair and pain. In the final analysis each of us has to surrender our body. Some people through illness or disability have the courage to do this while they live.

Despite the volunteer schemes attached to most institutions, the opportunities for either housebound or institutionalized people to meet, as one woman put it, 'like minded people', are few and far between. If each one of us who is mobile was able to extend a hand of friendship, both sides would gain.

Friendship networks could prevent patronage or mismatch. A two-way scheme to enable people to meet like-minded people could go something like this. Anyone joining the register, mobile or immobile, would be invited to write a brief description of themselves, their interests, politics, outlook on life and so on. The information would be collated and circulated. The housebound or incapacitated member of the network would then be able to choose their preferred visitor. If the first introduction did not work, the register could be referred to again. In order to safeguard housebound people living on their own, a co-ordinator would need to meet participants first. Only one generous person is needed to initiate a pilot scheme of this nature.

If you are housebound or living in an institution and find yourself with few or no friends, make a fuss. Write an article and send it to a national paper. Ring up the press. Spell out what you need. This is not a complaint, it is having respect for the life in you. Shout it from the rooftops: 'Where is my other family?'

Attitudes towards disability are changing very slowly thanks to an articulate minority of socially and politically motivated people with disabilities. These people firmly reject the stereotypes that have surrounded them for so long. They look upon their disability as part of themselves; not that they are people in spite of their disability. Nevertheless many disabled people are still very lonely. Is it surprising when so little is done to help people who are disabled to be part of the social stream? Access remains a huge problem: pavements without ramps, buildings without lifts, lack of suitable transport, lavatories that are too small for a wheelchair – the list is endless. What could be more lonely than having to plan a visit to the cinema as if it were an expedition to the Himalayas?

Do we welcome disabled people as part of the community? The answer is 'no'. We see the disability rather than the person. One nurse described how she and a few of her disabled friends headed for the local pub to have a celebratory Christmas drink. The publican quietly asked the nurse (please note, nurse – not the others) to ask them to drink up and leave. 'Nothing personal, I just don't want to upset my other customers.'

Should the reward of being proudly independent, living a normal working life despite the disadvantage of not being able to see, or not being able to hear, or having a physical deformity, be social isolation? Isolation because of public indifference, ignorance or fear. Organizations run by disabled people working to ensure they are a voice in society always welcome new members. If you feel like joining one or setting up your own group don't waste time, join now (*see* Useful Addresses). Disabled people, like other minority groups, are now proudly developing their own philosophy and culture. If they continue to be left on the fringes of society we will all lose out.

CHAPTER TWELVE

Conclusions

The end of the book? Yes, but for you and me it is really just the beginning. In order to be truly free we need to work on ourselves right up until the day we die. This process could be likened to peeling an onion. One layer is uncovered only to reveal another. Working on ourselves means living in the moment, being aware, infinitely patient and infinitely kind.

The starting point of this book was the suggestion that, in order to work through any problem, it is necessary to start from where we are right now rather than where we want to be. Most of us have in mind our model of a perfect being or someone we have cast in the role of mentor. Oh, the loneliness and conflict when we realize that we cannot fly over the moon or overnight walk through life as our 'perfect being' does.

The first step towards transcending any problem and the first step towards real freedom is the realization that there is no need to suppress any negative thought, fear, state or sensation. When negative thoughts arise, fearlessly and impartially observe them until they go their way. There is no need to fight or punish ourselves. All we can do is our best at that particular moment. Each step forwards is worth one hundred steps backwards.

Perhaps at the beginning you were hoping the book would focus on where to go, what to do, and how to meet people. Instead it has concentrated mainly on the preliminary work that needs to be done before external solutions are sought. Loneliness is not your failure or my failure. It is a common condition and largely a Western phenomenon. The experience

of loneliness is an opportunity for personal growth. In order
to work through this state and see it in that light it is necessary
to come to terms with and define our own loneliness, to look
inwards first.

Once you and I are no longer afraid of loneliness, we are
on our way to walking with life in a more magnificent state,
that of the alone. You and I, the alone, enjoy both people and
solitude. We flow with both the good times and the not so
good times. We do belong, we are here for a reason, though
what it is we may never understand. We are not a forgotten
pea mistakenly left by itself in a pod. We are part of the family
of life. We are part of nature.

Live in the moment and use the exercises for moments of
acute pain. Remind yourself each day you are your own person; work on the art of communication. Give each and every
one moment by moment attention. Live less in the head and
more in the body. Look for your other family. Follow your
'bliss'. Go for it.

Now it is time to take the initiative and share the brightness
of your heart with other people. No longer allow yourself
to be sealed in by the habit or hurt of loneliness. Taking
the initiative means risk. Let go imagined security, the
familiar which however painful seems preferable to the
unknown. If what you are seeking does not at first materialize
do not give up. Be positive. Ask that you be pointed in
the right direction. Good things will happen, sometimes in
the most unexpected way.

PRACTICAL SUGGESTIONS

The following suggestions are offered simply as a starting
point for an individual quest. Details of all the publications
and organizations mentioned will be found in either the
Further Reading or Useful Addresses Sections.

To point yourself in the right direction draw up a list of the
things you would like to do that will bring contact with other
people. Write down all your ideas from the possible to the
seemingly impossible. Really think about it. What do you
enjoy, what would you like to do but are too shy or afraid

to try out? What kind of people would you like to meet? Are you looking for a partner or new friends? Are you looking for just one new like-minded friend? Do you need therapeutic support? If so, consider in what form. It really helps to make a plan. You can tick off the items each time you step out and this will give you courage and help you not to retreat.

Directories are an excellent source of information. The Further Reading list recommends a number of useful ones covering different subjects. Yellow pages, local papers, libraries and Citizens' Advice Bureaux are also useful sources of local information.

Introduction agencies and singles clubs

Many people young and old say they would find it very difficult if not impossible to pluck up courage and approach an introduction agency with the idea of meeting a partner: 'I just couldn't . . . too shy . . . seems like a last resort . . . don't think you should, it doesn't seem right to do it that way'. If the idea of meeting new people in this way is not for you, it is not for you. However, it is worth considering introduction agencies briefly before dismissing them. The present structures of our society does not afford everyone easy opportunities to meet new people. Responsible agencies or singles clubs have the potential to be able to fill this gap, particularly now that more people are realizing this is a logical way to make contact.

Asking a professional organization to link us up with other people needs to become acceptable in our own minds. There are sincere and reputable introduction agencies which genuinely wish to introduce the right people to each other. They have a high success rate in enabling people to have a wider circle of friends or find a partner. Agencies who meet their clients are recommended. Obviously a face-to-face encounter enables the interviewer to become more aware of the personality and essence of a person. The Association of British Introduction Agencies has a code of practice and advises people to use only agencies that are members.

One young woman who joined an introduction agency failed to find the perfect partner, but gained a new set of friends: 'Once we got the partnership thing out of the way we found we had many common interests.' Maybe she was lucky, or may be she was wise enough not to write the whole thing off as failure just because the partnership she was seeking did not materialize.

Margaret Nelson's book *Someone to Love* gives information and advice on seeking friendship through the personal columns.

Singles clubs or singles activities are again a sensible and logical way to meet new people. One person interviewed said in their experience they were 'too commercially orientated'. Yes, they are set up as a business but, provided they offer a sincere and welcoming service that brings people together, does that matter? Usually clubs have free introductory evenings. Why not attend one: there is absolutely nothing to lose. Clubs ask for a subscription but it is often refundable before the end of the first month. It really is worth finding out about singles clubs and their particular focus. One man joined a club with a European focus. He attended the French conversation evenings. They met in a wine bar. 'If I hadn't had the excuse of practising French I wouldn't have had the courage to go.'

If you find clubs are not the answer please don't put yourself down or retreat and give up the attempt to build a social life. There are many other routes to explore which may be more sympathetic to your nature.

Setting up a Group

Starting up a group yourself can bring you contact with all sorts of people. Not only that, you are making a social contribution. Whether you want to start a group or meet one or two people with whom you can exchange skills or share interests, the best place to advertise is in a national or local paper, the library, a local education college or a relevant magazine. If you get a group going it is wise to start by holding a monthly meeting. Members could take turns to offer hospitality. It need not be a formal arrangement. Here are some ideas:

A friendship network to put people with common
interests in touch

Exchanging skills; for example 'willing to teach Spanish
in exchange for learning to play the guitar'

A correspondence club for a specialized interest

A monthly discussion/debating group (topics to be
decided upon in advance)

A chess, bridge, model-making or any other specialized-
interest group

A regular exchange between one or two people

A book club

A gardening or allotment club

A writing group – try out ideas and be prepared for
criticism

A kite club

A meditation group; invite a skilled teacher to lead the
group at least once a month

A loneliness support group.

Setting up a self-help group with people supporting each
other through a particular difficulty requires thought. The
Council for Voluntary Service and The Self Help Team
offer excellent information packs on how to get started and
the pitfalls.

Voluntary work

Voluntary work is a lot more than helping out charities. It is
a marvellous way to broaden one's horizons and come into
contact with many different people. Volunteers are welcomed
in hospitals, arts centres, political and environmental groups,
counselling projects, or busy organizations. If you would like
to be involved with a particular project or organization write
to them direct even if they have not advertised for volunteers.
Occasionally people who have offered to be volunteers find
themselves invited to become part of an organization. Volunteer bureaux have lists of places where volunteers are needed.
The Volunteer Bureaux Directory gives information on local
bureaux. Volunteering holidays present the opportunity to
make a contribution and have fun.

Further education

Further education colleges and polytechnics offer a range of courses which seem to grow year by year. It is possible to learn practically anything. Age is no limit neither is lack of formal qualifications. You can learn to massage, be a liberated male or female, understand Chinese calligraphy, be assertive, or take an A level. Whatever you learn, you will also meet other people in a relaxed and informal way.

Correspondence courses are exciting and challenging. They can be lifelines for people who are housebound or living in remote areas. The Useful Addresses list, under 'Further Education', gives information on correspondence courses. For information on local colleges consult the local education authority, library or telephone directory.

Artistic activities

Enjoying the arts, or actively participating in them, can re-kindle a spark of fun. Life can take on a new dimension when we discover or rediscover our creative potential. Learn to paint, design, dance, act, make music, write. Many arts centres have excellent education programmes for adults as well as children. Often they are poorly publicized so you need to ring up their education department. Many smaller arts centres welcome volunteers to help in the café or just generally.

Sport

The Sports Council has information on local activities. Try out new forms of exercise, swim or join a walking club. Start a club if there is nothing locally. Exercise in its many forms can help to dissolve moments of loneliness.

Holidays

More and more people are taking holidays alone. Make sure that if you do you hold your head up high and don't take any rubbish from the holiday booking clerk or the staff where you are staying. Sit where you want, do what you want to and ask for what you want, particularly since you have to pay a supplement for going on holiday alone and taking up a single room.

Group holidays with a purpose are the easiest to begin with, for example trekking, skiing, walking or volunteering holidays. Therapeutic/holistic holiday centres provide opportunities to meet new people who are also searching to expand themselves. If these ideas seem too daunting consider participating in a retreat which may well provide the refreshment you need. The Further Reading and Useful Addresses list provide information on holidays for people who are older or disabled, retreat centres and volunteering holidays.

If you are someone who finds family holidays difficult because they make too many demands try going off on your own for space and quietness. Reassure your family in such a way that they do not feel rejected. Offer your partner the opportunity to do the same.

THERAPEUTIC SUPPORT

Never feel you have to work through loneliness alone. There are many people to whom you can turn for support. Often it is easier to talk to a counsellor or therapist than someone you know. The British Association for Counselling publishes a directory of qualified counsellors and psychotherapists. They also send out local information on receipt of a stamped addressed envelope. The Westminster Pastoral Foundation is another source of information and Liz Hodgkinson's book *Counselling* answers many of the questions people have about this subject as well as giving advice on how to find a properly trained counsellor.

Joining a self-help group can be a way to find support, perhaps one of the best ways. Unfortunately there are few if any which specifically address the subject of loneliness. If you decide to start one it is guaranteed there will be no shortage of members.

Learning to do something healing, for example learning to massage, counsel or run a group, is a way of not only helping others, but also ourselves.

Exercise is therapeutic, particularly movement that is based on balancing the body, such as Tai chi, yoga and the Alexander Technique. Further education colleges often offer classes in these forms of movement (*see also* Useful Addresses).

Learning to meditate can be of great benefit. If possible learn under the guidance of a skilled teacher. Should you decide to take this route, meditate if possible at least once a week with the group and regularly on your own for half to one hour each day. Meditating only when the going gets rough doesn't really work. The self-help/psychology and religion sections of bookshops are good places to browse through for books on meditation.

The course is over. Perhaps in the final analysis none of us truly knows what we are searching for. Lasting peace of mind and happiness can only come from within. When you and I find this for ourselves no person, situation or event can ever take it away. May you and I go well.

Appendix: Others' Perspectives on Loneliness

Let us approach this problem again to see what is actually taking place, to see what you do when you feel lonely. You try to escape from your feeling of loneliness, you try to get on with a book, you follow some leader, or you go to a cinema, or you become socially very, very active, or you go and worship and pray, or you paint, or you write a poem about loneliness . . . Have you ever tried to be alone? When you do try, you will feel how extraordinarily difficult it is and how extraordinarily intelligent we must be to be alone, because the mind will not let us be alone . . . We are trying to fill this extraordinary void with the known . . . We try to fill that emptiness with various kinds of knowledge, relationship or things . . . You have tried every means of filling this void of loneliness . . . Have you succeeded in filling it or have you merely covered it up? If you have merely covered it up, it is still there; therefore it will come back . . . How then will you find what to do about this loneliness? You can only find what to do when you have stopped escaping . . . When you are willing to face what *is* – which means you must not turn on the radio, which means you must turn your back to civilisation – then that loneliness comes to an end, because it is completely transformed. It is no longer loneliness. If you understand what *is* then what *is* is the real . . . When you see what *is*, you will find how loneliness is transformed.

J Krishnamurti, *The First and Last Freedom*

Until we have nothing to hide, we cannot be free. If we are still considering the contents of the mind as the enemy, we become frightened, thinking we have something especially wrong with us.

Not recognising the mind as just the result of previous conditioning, nothing special. That all these states of mind which we fear so much can actually be mulched back into ourselves to become fertiliser, the manure for further growth. Which means that in order to allow these materials to compost, to become rich fertilisers for growth, we must begin to make room in our hearts for ourselves. We must begin to cultivate the compassion that allows the moment to be as it is, in the clear light of awareness, without the least postponement of the truth.

. . . And we begin to penetrate the surface commotion and find that guilt and fear and anger, and all the mental smorgasbord that has been stashed there, are nothing to be afraid of. We imagine that these things we have suppressed are who we really are. But by starting to acknowledge these qualities, to bring them into awareness, to open to them with some compassion for this human condition we find ourselves in, allows us to go deeper to what underlies this seemingly solid reality. As long as we are pushing parts of ourselves away, we cannot go deeper. 'Self-knowledge is bad news,' as a frightened friend put it. Or as one Tibetan teacher said of the penetration of this layer of suppressed material, 'It is just one insult after another'. Most people are afraid of confronting all the stuff they have pushed down because they still think of it as being who they are. We are frightened of all the forbidden mind states that we have pushed below the surface of awareness to protect our self-image.

Yet we see that we must suppress nothing. In suppression we push below what we imagine is unacceptable. In this very act of suppressing we enslave ourselves. We have postponed life once again. Nothing can be free of its prison of darkness until it has been brought out into the light of awareness. Suppression pushes things out of awareness where they become inaccessible. Tendencies that motivate us are still present but we no longer have access to them because they have been forced below the level of awareness. So each feeling must be acknowledged in its turn, allowed to exist without judgment or fear in clear awareness where it may be seen for what it is, an impermanent, oddly impersonal state of mind passing through. We imagine that we are caught in some unworkable situation, that life is a punishment instead of a gift.

Stephen Levine, *Who Dies?*

You begin to see that there are seasons in your life in the same way as there are seasons in nature. There are times to cultivate and create, when you nurture your world and give birth to new ideas and ventures. There are times of flourishing and abundance, when life feels in full bloom, energised and expanding. And there are times of fruition, when things come to an end. They have reached their climax and must be harvested before they begin to fade. And finally, of course, there are times that are cold and cutting and empty, times when the spring of new beginnings seems like a distant dream. Those rhythms in life are natural events. They weave into one another as day follows night, bringing, not messages of hope and fear, but messages of how things are. If you realise that each phase of your life is a natural occurrence, then you need not be swayed, pushed up and down by the changes in circumstance and mood that life brings. You find that you have an opportunity to be fully in the world at all times and to show yourself as a brave and proud individual in any circumstance.

Chögyam Trungpa, *The Sacred Path of the Warrior*

Heaven and earth are impartial,
    they regard all creatures as sacred.
The self-controlled man is impartial,
    he regards all people as sacred.

The space between Heaven and Earth is like a bellows.
    Emptied, it loses not power,
    Moved, it sends forth more and more wind.

    Many words lead to exhaustion.
    Be not thus; keep to thy centre.

Lao Tzü, *Tao Teh King*

The greatest healing in the world is being yourselves.

Reshad Feild, *Breathing Alive*

Do not weep; do not wax indignant. Understand.

Baruch Spinoza

Even a happy life cannot be without a measure of darkness and the word 'happiness' would lose its meaning if it were not balanced by sadness.

C.G. Jung

The miracle is not to fly in the air, or to walk on the water, but to walk on the earth.

Chinese proverb

Every blade of grass has its Angel that bends over it and whispers, 'Grow, grow.'

The Talmud

Rather light a candle than complain about the darkness.

Chinese proverb

We do not see things as they are. We see them as we are.

The Talmud

God grant me the serenity to accept the things I cannot change, courage to change the things I can, and wisdom to know the difference.

Reinhold Niebuhr

What lies behind us, and what lies before us are tiny matters, compared to what lies within us.

Ralph Waldo Emerson

The mark of your ignorance is the depth of your belief in injustice and tragedy. What the caterpillar calls the end of the world, the master calls a butterfly.

Richard Bach

Turn your face to the sun and the shadows fall behind you.

Maori proverb

> I do my thing, and you do your thing,
> I am not in this world to live up to your expectations
> And you are not in this world to live up to mine.
> You are you and I am I,
> And if by chance we find each other, it's beautiful.
> If not, it can't be helped.

Frederick S. Perls

O Master, make me not so much to be consoled as to console; not so much to be loved as to love; not so much to be understood as to understand; for it is in giving that one receives, it is in self-forgetfulness that one finds; it is in pardoning that one is pardoned; it is in dying that one finds eternal life.

Christian prayer

I sometimes think I love everything and Everybody But I know I don't. (Soraya aged 9)

Love . . . it makes you coff a lot. (Peter aged 5)

Once I saw a Christmas tree being put to death. (Sally aged 8)

My big sister fell in love and she went to this place where they sell you holy matrimony but I don't think she paid them all the money because she said it wasn't worth it. (Malcolm aged 7)

Guinea Pigs Like Peace. (Emma aged 4)

Nanette Newman, *God Bless Love*

References

1 Swimme, Brian, in *Soul*, BBC.
2 Schwarz, Joe, in *The Guardian*, 13 June 1992.
3 Hindmarch, Carl, 'Sobs for the Boys', in *The Guardian*, 30 June
  1992.

Further Reading

BOOKS

Bly, Robert, *Iron John*, Element, 1991.
Encourages men to explore who they are rather than who they think they should be.

Dennet, Daniel, *Consciousness Explained*, A Lane, 1992.

Dowrick, Stephanie, *Intimacy and Solitude: Balancing Closeness and Independence*, Women's Press, 1992.

Feild, Reshad, *Breathing Alive*, Element, 1988.

Fontana, David, *The Elements of Meditation*, Element, 1991.
— *The Meditator's Handbook*, Element, 1992.

Hanh, Thich Nhat, *The Heart of Understanding*, Parallax Press, California, 1988.
— *The Miracle of Mindfulness*, Rider 1991.
Meditation for daily life; by Buddhist teacher but suitable for people of any faith or none.

Hay, Louise, *You Can Heal Your Life*, Eden Grove Editions, 1988.
An excellent book for encouraging a positive approach to living.

Hodgkinson, Liz, *Counselling*, Simon & Schuster, 1992.
Answers the difficult questions people have about counselling; explains different styles of counselling and how to find properly trained counsellors.
— *Happy to be Single*, Thorsons, 1993

Jeffers, Susan, *Feel the Fear and Do It Anyway*, Arrow Books, 1991.
Explains how to work through fear to a resolution.

Kelley, Kevin (ed.), *The Home Planet*, McDonald Queen Anne Press, 1988.

Kiley, Dr Dan, *Living Together and Feeling Alone*, Cedar, 1991. For women to overcome hidden loneliness within a relationship.

Krishnamurti, J., *The First and Last Freedom*, Victor Gollancz, 1978.
— *Meditation*, Shambhala Pocket Classics, 1991.

Levine, Stephen, *Who Dies?*, Gateway Books, 1986. An investigation of conscious living and conscious dying.

Nelson, Margaret, *Someone to Love: How to find romance in the personal column*, Sheldon Press, 1990.

Newman, Mildred, and Berhowiz, Bernard, with Owen, Jean, *How to be Your Own Best Friend*, Cedar, 1991.

Newman, Nanette, *God Bless Love*, Collins, 1972.

Peck, Alan, *An Introduction to Tai Chi*, McDonald Optima, 1990. Tai chi, originally a system of self-defence, is a subtle form of movement for students of any age which promotes flexibility, harmony and balance. Book contains addresses of local centres.

Peiffer, Vera, *Positively Single: The art of being single and happy*, Element, 1991.

Seidler, Victor, *Men, Sex and Relationships*, Routledge, 1992. Written for men to help them deal with their relationships with women and their families.

Sumedho, Venerable Ajahn, *Mindfulness, The Path to the Deathless*, Amaravati Publications, 1987.
— *Seeing the Way*, Amaravati Publications, 1987.
Meditation teaching; by Buddhist teacher but suitable for people of any faith or none.

Suzuki-roshi, Shunryu, *Zen Mind, Beginner's Mind*, Weatherhill, New York, 1973.
By Buddhist teacher but suitable for people of any faith or none.

Trungpa, Chögyam, *The Sacred Path of the Warrior*, Shambhala, 1984.

Tzü, Lao, *Tao Teh King*, Theosophical Publishing House, 1983.

DIRECTORIES

Addresses of most of the organizations mentioned below will be found in the next section, Useful Addresses.

Arts Council, *The Arts and Disability Directory* (£5 and £7 incl. p & p) .
National information for disabled people who want to become involved in the arts and for anyone wanting to become involved in this area of work.

Bedford Press, *Networking in Europe*, Plymbridge Distributors, Plymouth.
A guide to voluntary organizations in Europe.

British Association for Counselling, *The British Association and Psychotherapy Resources Directory* (£17).
Lists registered psychotherapists, psychoanalysts and counsellors. Sheets of local information free on request with SAE.

Buddhist Society, *The Buddhist Directory* (£5).
Lists Buddhist centres throughout UK.

Cruse, *Holiday Ideas from Cruse for People Holidaying Alone.*
Some 150 ideas, from a house party in Portugal to a chance to learn.

Gale Research, *The Encyclopedia of Associations.*
US directory of voluntary, support, non-profit-making and charitable organizations; available in UK reference libraries and US public libraries.

Marc Europe, *The UK Christian Handbook* (£25 excl. p & p).
Also available in most public libraries. Lists some 500 Christian organizations plus accommodation in guest houses, hotels etc.

National Association of Volunteer Bureaux, *The Volunteer Bureaux Directory*, W & R Chambers (£6).

National Council of Voluntary Organisations, *The Voluntary Agencies Directory*, Bedford Square Press (£10.95).
Lists some 2,000 national voluntary organizations; of interest to anyone considering volunteer work.

Saur, K.G., *The Year Book of International Associations.*
Lists voluntary, charitable and non-profit-making associations; available in reference libraries.

Sports Council, *The Sports Council Governing Bodies Address Book*. Local information sheets free on request with SAE. Useful information on sports and keep fit.

Whiteaker, Stafford, *The Good Retreat Guide*, Rider (£9.99). Some 2,000 places to find peace and quiet.

Youth Hostels Association, *Accommodation Guide, England and Wales* (free on membership).
— *Guide to Budget Accommodation, Europe and Mediterranean* (£6.55).
— *Guide to Budget Accommodation, Africa, Asia and Australasia* (£6.55).

Young Men's Christian Association, *The World Wide Directory of YMCAs*.

Useful Addresses

Many of these organizations publish directories – *see* Further Reading.

ARTS

The Arts Council of Great
   Britain
14 Great Peter Street
London SW1P 3NQ
071 333 0100

For national information contact the Arts Council. For local information contact your Regional Arts Board.

BEREAVEMENT

Cruse – Bereavement Care
Cruse House
126 Sheen Road
Richmond
Surrey TW9 1UR
081 940 4818

Offers counselling, advice and opportunities for social contact to all bereaved people.

Jewish Bereavement
   Counselling Service
1 Cyprus Gardens
London WC1
071 387 4300 ext. 227
081 349 0839 (24-hour
   answerphone)

Support for members of the Jewish community who have been bereaved, and a resource and information centre to both the Jewish and non-Jewish community in London and the rest of the UK.

COUNSELLING AND THERAPY

The Archway Foundation
9 Green Ridges
Headington
Oxford OX3 9PL
0865 790552

Provides support and
counselling specifically to
relieve loneliness. The other
branch is in Rotherham, South
Yorkshire.

British Association for
   Counselling
1 Regent Place
Rugby
Warwickshire CU21 2PJ
0788 578328

Relate: National Marriage
   Guidance
Herbert Gray College
Little Church Street
Rugby
Warwickshire CV21 3AP
0788 573241

Co-ordinates about 160 local
Relate centres which undertake
education in personal
relationships, and counselling
for those seeking help in
marriage and family

relationships and sexual
problems.

Samaritans
17 Uxbridge Road
Slough
Berkshire SL1 1SN
0753 532713

Helps the suicidal and
despairing. There are 183
Samaritan branches in the UK
and Irish Republic. Local
helplines are listed in the front
of telephone directories.

Befrienders International
228 Bishops Gate
London EC2M 4QD

Provides information on
international branches of
Samaritans and similar
projects.

Westminster Pastoral
   Foundation
23 Kensington Square
London W8 5HN
071 937 6956

Provides information and
counselling services.

FOR PEOPLE WITH DISABILITIES OR WHO ARE HOUSEBOUND

Arts Organizations

Artsline
5 Crowndale Road
London NW1 1TU
071 388 2227
071 387 387 5911

Provides information and advice to disabled people on all aspects of the arts and leisure activities in Greater London. Telephone information and advice service.

Disability Arts magazine
DAM Publishing
10 Woad Lane
Grimsby DN37 9NH
0472 280031

Publishes national quarterly magazine promoting arts for disabled people. News, information, access. Yearly subscription £12, unwaged £6.

Shape London and Shape Network, HAI, USA
See under 'For Older People'.

European Association for Creativity for Disabled People
Eucrea Sq. Ambiorix 32
B. 1040 Brussels
Belgium

Other Organizations

British Council of Organisations of Disabled People (BCODP)
St Mary's Church
Greenlaw Street
London SE18 5AR
081 316 4184

A national umbrella organization made up of national, regional and local groups and organizations run and controlled by disabled people to unite the voice of disabled people. They encourage and support links

between new and existing self-help groups.

Mobility International
228 Borough High Street
London SE1 1JX

Runs international projects for disabled people aged eighteen to thirty.

National Listening Library
12 Lant Street
London SE1 1QR
071 407 9417

Provides a postal lending library service of literature recorded on long-playing cassettes for the benefit of people who are unable to read in the conventional way. 'Talking books' are played on special cassette players supplied on free loan. There is a contribution of £15 a year towards the cost of the service. Financial assistance may be obtained.

National Tape Magazine for the Blind
105 Salisbury Road
London NW6 6RH
071 624 8844

Provides the visually impaired with recordings of articles of interest which are normally found in the wide variety of printed magazines available to the general public.

Sympathetic Hearing Scheme
7–11 Armstrong Road
London W3 7JL
081 740 4447

Provides support and encouragement to hearing-impaired people who face problems when trying to listen in public places.

Winged Fellowship Trust
(Holidays and Respite Care for
  Disabled People)
Angel House
20–32 Pentonville Road
London N1 9XD
071 833 2594

Provides holidays and respite care for severely physically disabled people and offers opportunities for voluntary service to men and women of all ages and nationalities.

EDUCATION

For information on local adult education centres and programmes consult your telephone directory, library, Citizens' Advice Bureau or local authority education department.

Council for the Accreditation
  of Correspondence Colleges
27 Marylebone Road
London NW1 5JS
071 935 5391

Provides advice and information on accredited courses.

National Extension College
18 Brooklands Avenue
Cambridge CB2 2HH
0223 31664

Provides further education correspondence courses for students from the age of 14 to 90, who would like to get into higher education professional training, or simply wish to study because they enjoy it. Wide range of subjects to study. Write for brochure of courses available. No previous qualifications needed.

Open University
PO Box 200
Milton Keynes
Buckinghamshire MK7 6Y2

Offers degree and a wide range of further education courses by correspondence.

University of the Third Age (U3A)
1 Stockwell Green
London SW9 9JF
071 737 2541

Promotes self-help educational activities among retired people of all ages. Supports new and existing self-help groups.

HEALTH

Help for Health
Grant Building
Southampton General Hospital
Southampton SO9 4XY
0703 779 091
0703 777 222 ext. 6653

Houses database information of 1,000 voluntary organizations and self-help groups mainly in the West Country, Wiltshire, Dorset, Hampshire, Isle of Wight. Also has extensive information on London self-help projects.

MIND
(National Association for Mental Health)
22 Harley Street
London W1N 2ED
071 637 0741

Aims to promote the interests and views of people suffering from mental distress in all its many forms. Provides information through its London headquarters and 200 local associations.

The World Federation For Mental Health
The Secretariat
1021 Prince Street
Alexandria
Virginia 22314
USA

Co-ordinator for Europe
34 Swains Lane
London N6 6QR

Provides international information on mental health organizations.

HOLIDAYS

Cortijo Romero Holistic
  Holidays
Cortijo Romero
Aptdo De Correos 31
Orgiva
Granada 18400
Spain

Runs different therapeutic /
holistic holidays / courses.

Countrywide Holidays
  Association
Birch Heys
Cromwell Range
Manchester M14 6HU
061 225 1000

Walking and other activity
holidays in Britain and abroad.
Group, family, singles.

HF Holidays
Imperial House
Edgware Road
Colindale
London NW9 5AL
081 905 9556

Encourage walking holidays.
Organizes a varied programme
of special interest holidays in

Britain and abroad, from
bridge to bird watching.

Holiday Care Service
2 Old Bank Chambers
Station Road
Horley
Surrey RH6 8HW
0293 774535

Holiday information service to
give free advice to anyone
who, because of disability or
other special needs or family
circumstances, has difficulty in
finding a suitable holiday.

Saga Holidays plc
Middleburg Square
Folkestone
Kent CT20 1AZ
0303 857000

Specializes in holidays for
people over 60.

The Skyros Centre
92 Prince of Wales Road
London NW5 3NE
071 267 4424

Runs a holistic holiday centre
on the Greek island of Skyros.

FOR OLDER PEOPLE

Age Concern England
  (National Council on
  Ageing)
1268 London Road
London SW16 4EJ
081 679 8000

Aims to improve the quality of
life for older people, in
particular to campaign on
issues relating to them.
Provides older people with
information and advice.

Age Endeavour Fellowship
Willowthorpe
High Street
Stanstead Abbots
Nr Ware
Hertfordshire SG12 8AS
0920 870158

Provides employment and
activities for retired and elderly
people. Over 200 Employment
Fellowship Centres have been
set up.

Help the Aged
16–18 St James's Walk
London EC1R OBE
071 253 0253

A national charity which aims
to improve the quality of life
of elderly people in the UK
and overseas.

Help Age International
rue Froissard 123
B. 1040 Brussels
Belgium

Eurolink Age
rue du Trône 98
B. 1050 Brussels
Belgium

Links older people from
different countries to speak for
the rights of older people.

Reach
89 Southwark Street
London SE1 OHD
071 928 0452

Brings together retired
executives from business and
industry (and particularly those
who retire early) to work on
an expenses-only basis for
charities, voluntary
organizations or community
groups which need but cannot
afford their specialists skills.

University of the Third Age
(U3A)
1 Stockwell Green
London SW9 9JF
071 737 2541

Promotes self-help educational
activities among retired people
of all ages. Supports new and
existing self-help groups.

Shape London
1 Thorpe Close
London W10 5XL
081 960 9245 (main office)
081 960 9249 (ticket scheme)

Operates a theatre/concert
ticket scheme for elderly and
disabled people.

Shape Network
c/o East Midlands Shape
27a Belvoir Street
Leicester LE1 6FL

The SHAPE Network is a
federation of eighteen local
services. The services work to
increase access and
involvement of disabled,
elderly and other under-
represented groups in all

aspects of the arts. For further information contact your nearest SHAPE service or SHAPE Network in Leicester.

HAI (Hospital Audiences Inc)
220 West 42 Street
New York
New York 10036
USA

Organization making the arts more accessible for ill, disabled, elderly or deprived people.

RELIGION

Amaravati Buddhist Centre
Great Gaddesden
Hemel Hempstead
Hertfordshire HP1 3BZ
0442 842 455

Runs workshops, meditation, retreats, summer family camp; welcomes guests.

Findhorn Foundation
The Park
Forres
Scotland IV36 OTZ
0309 30311

Works for the advancement of spiritual and religious studies. Runs residential educational programmes and conferences, organizes workshops for Findhorn community members and guests.

Friends of the Western Buddhist Order,
London Buddhist Centre
51 Roman Road
London E2 OHU
081 981 1225

Organizes meditation courses, Buddhist retreats, classes in yoga and other Eastern forms of controlled movement.

The Buddhist Society
58 Eccleston Square
London SW1V 1PH
071 834 5858

Provides information on schools of Buddhism, talks, correspondence courses, meditation. Publishes quarterly magazine *Middle Way*.

Christian Churches Council for Health and Healing
St Marylebone Parish Church
Marylebone Road
London NW1
071 486 9644

Interfaith Network for the UK
5/7 Tavistock Place
London WC1
071 388 0008

Marc Europe
Vision Building
4 Footscray Road
Eltham
London SE9 2TZ

Publishes Christian Handbook listing 5,000 Christian organizations, accommodation, guest houses.

Religious Society of Friends (Quakers),
Friends House
Euston Road
London NW1 2BJ

The social and international activities of the society spring from its conviction that religious witness involves continuing concern for the needs of all people.

SOCIAL

Local information on social activities should be listed in local papers, libraries and Citizens' Advice Bureaux.

Association of British
   Introduction Agencies
25 Abingdon Road
London W8 6AL
071 938 1011

Acts as an intermediary between member introduction agencies and the public. Has a code of practice and a list of agencies belonging to it.

Gingerbread
35 Wellington Street
London WC2E 7BN
071 240 0953

Provides practical help and social activities for lone parents and their children via a national network of local self-help groups.

National Federation of
Women's Institutes
104 New Kings Road
London SW6 4LY
071 371 9300

Aims to improve and develop conditions of rural life and to advance the education of countrywomen in citizenship.

Outsiders Club
PO Box 42B
London W1A 4ZB
071 837 3559

Invites disabled people to be in touch with each other.

'Stylopal' Braille Pen Pal Club
c/o Civic Centre
Newcastle-upon-Tyne
   NE1 8PA
091 232 8520 ext. 6320

Arranges for Braillists to contact others in the world. Prospective members should state age, date of birth, grade of Braille, interests and hobbies.

Townswomen's Guilds
Chamber of Commerce House

75 Harborne Road
Birmingham B15 3DA
021 456 3435

Provides a common meeting ground for social and recreational pursuits, with a view to improving the conditions of life for women.

SPORTS AND FITNESS

Alexander Technique Society
  of Teachers (STAT)
20 London House
266 Fulham Road
London SW10 9EL
071 351 0828

For information on the Alexander Technique send SAE.

Keep Fit Association
16 Upper Woburn Place
London WC1H OQP
071 387 4349

Iyengar Yoga Institute
223a Randolph Avenue
London W9 1NL
071 624 3080

Advances public education in the classical teachings of the science of yoga. Provides information about centres throughout UK and abroad.

The Sports Council
  Headquarters
16 Upper Woburn Place
London WC1H OQP
071 388 1277

VOLUNTARY AND SELF-HELP ORGANIZATIONS

The National Council for
  Voluntary Organisations
  (NCVO)
Regents Wharf
All Saints Street
London N1 9RL
071 713 6161

Leading voluntary agency. Excellent source of information on voluntary groups.

The Independent Sector
(Philanthropy)
1828L Street NW
Washington DC 20036
USA

Provides US information and
supports the work of the
voluntary sector.

International Council of
Voluntary Agencies (ICVA)
rue Gautier 13
CH 1201 Geneva
Switzerland

Amnesty International
British Section
99–119 Rosebery Avenue
London EC1R 4RE
071 278 6000

International Secretariat
1 Easton Street
London WC1X 8DJ

A worldwide human rights
movement. Welcomes
volunteers.

British Trust for Conservation
Volunteers
36 St Mary's Street
Wallingford
Oxfordshire OX10 OEU
0491 39766

Volunteer working holidays in
the UK and Europe. Write for
brochure.

Council for Voluntary Service
13 Hazelwood Road
Northampton NH1 1LG
0604 241 21

Offers self-help action pack
giving detailed advice on
setting up a self-help group,
and other information.

National Association of
Volunteer Bureaux
St Peter's College
College Road
Saltley
Birmingham B8 3TE
021 327 0265

Reach
See under 'For Older People'.

Samaritans
17 Uxbridge Road
Slough
Berkshire SL1 1SN
0753 32713

Trains volunteers to respond
to helplines.

Self-Help Centre
Regents Wharf
8 All Saints Street
London N1 9RL
071 713 6161

Provides general national self-
help information.

The Self-Help Team
20 Pelhorn Road
Sherwood Rise
Nottingham NG5 1AP

Provides an information pack
'Starting Off' which gives clear
details of how to set up a self-
help group (price £4).

International Information
Centre on self-help and
health
E Van Evenstraat 2C
B. 3000 Leuven
Belgium

GENERAL

Alzheimer's Disease Society
158–60 Balham High Road
London SW12 9BN
081 675 6557

Gives support to families by
linking them through
membership.

Capital Help Line
071 388 7575

Information and advice

Carers National Association
29 Chilworth Mews
London W2 3RG
071 724 7776

Aims to help anyone whose life
is in some way restricted
because of the need to take
care of a person who is ill.

Young Men's Christian
Association
Head Office
640 Forest Road
Walthamstow
London E17 3DZ

Budget accommodation world
wide.

Youth Hostels Association
Head Office
8 St Stephen's Hill
St Albans
Hertfordshire AL1 2DY
0727 55215

Annual subscription for those
aged over twenty £8.90; for
those aged sixteen to twenty
£4.70. Budget accommodation
UK, Europe, Africa,
Australasia.

Index